AN INTRODUCTION TO THE

HISTORY OF WOMEN'S SUFFRAGE

An Introduction to
the History of
Women's Suffrage

SUSAN B. ANTHONY

ELIZABETH CADY STANTON

MATILDA JOSLYN GAGE

IDA HUSTED HARPER

MILLLICENT FAWCETT

RENARD PRESS

RENARD PRESS LTD

Kemp House
152–160 City Road
London EC1V 2NX
United Kingdom
info@renardpress.com
020 8050 2928

www.renardpress.com

'Preface', 'Introduction', 'Chapter 1: Preceding Causes' and 'Appendix' first
published in *The History of Woman Suffrage*, Volume I in 1881
'Chapter 51: Progress of the Women's Movement in the United Kingdom' and
'Appendix: Nebraska Men's Association Opposed to Woman Suffrage' first pub-
lished in *The History of Woman Suffrage*, Volume VI in 1922
This edition first published by Renard Press Ltd in 2021

Edited text, notes and selection © Renard Press Ltd, 2021

Cover design by Will Dady

Printed in the United Kingdom by Severn

ISBN: 978-1-913724-64-1

9 8 7 6 5 4 3 2 1

CONTENTS

NOTE FROM THE PUBLISHER

The fight for the enfranchisement of women was a long and tortuous process, and yet it is today (fortunately) something that most are able to take for granted.

In 1881, when Susan B. Anthony, Elizabeth Cady Stanton and Matilda Joslyn Gage started to compile their *History of Woman Suffrage*, this certainly wasn't the case, and the idea of women and men, irrespective of class and skin colour, voting together and having an equal say in the running of their country was merely the stuff of dreams.

This little volume has as its foundation the opening essays of the first volume of the *History*, which gives a comprehensive overview of the leading names and battles on the road to enfranchisement (particularly in the United States), and takes in Millicent Fawcett's essay (from the final volume) on the battles on the British side of the pond, as well as an example of the depths of institutional misogyny these extraordinary women were faced with.

It is our hope that this volume can act as a helpful introduction to and overview of women's suffrage, and that it can stand as a celebration of the literary and democratic achievement of those who filled the pages of the *History*.

AN INTRODUCTION TO THE

HISTORY OF WOMEN'S SUFFRAGE

'Governments derive their just powers from the
consent of the governed.'*

Affectionately inscribed to the memory of

Mary Wollstonecraft, Frances Wright,
Lucretia Mott, Harriet Martineau, Lydia Maria Child,
Margaret Fuller, Sarah and Angelina Grimké,
Josephine S. Griffing, Martha C. Wright,
Harriot K. Hunt, MD, Mariana W. Johnson,
Alice and Phebe Cary, Ann Preston, MD,
Lydia Mott, Eliza W. Farnham, Lydia F. Fowler, MD,
Paulina Wright Davis,*

whose earnest lives and fearless words in demanding
political rights for women have been,
in the preparation of these pages,
a constant inspiration.

PREFACE

IN PREPARING THIS WORK,* our object has been
to put into permanent shape the few scattered
reports of the Woman Suffrage Movement* still
to be found, and to make it an arsenal of facts for those
who are beginning to inquire into the demands and
arguments of the leaders of this reform. Although the
continued discussion of the political rights of woman
during the last thirty years forms a most important link
in the chain of influences tending to her emancipation,
no attempt at its history has been made. In giving the
inception and progress of this agitation, we who have
undertaken the task have been moved by the consideration that many of our co-workers have already fallen
asleep, and that in a few years all who could tell the
story will have passed away.

In collecting material for these volumes, most of those
of whom we solicited facts have expressed themselves
deeply interested in our undertaking, and have gladly
contributed all they could, feeling that those identified
with this reform were better qualified to prepare a faithful

history with greater patience and pleasure than those of another generation possibly could.

A few have replied, 'It is too early to write the history of this movement – wait until our object is attained; the actors themselves cannot write an impartial history; they have had their discords, divisions, personal hostilities that unfit them for the work.' Viewing the enfranchisement of woman as the most important demand of the century, we have felt no temptation to linger over individual differences. These occur in all associations, and may be regarded in this case as an evidence of the growing self-assertion and individualism in woman.

Woven with the threads of this history, we have given some personal reminiscences and brief biographical sketches. To the few who, through ill-timed humility, have refused to contribute any of their early experiences, we would suggest that, as each brick in a magnificent structure might have had no special value alone on the roadside, yet, in combination with many others, its size, position, quality becomes of vital consequence; so with the actors in any great reform: though they may be of little value in themselves, as a part of a great movement they may be worthy of mention – even important to the completion of a historical record.

To be historians of a reform in which we have been among the chief actors has its points of embarrassment as well as advantage. Those who fight the battle can best give what all readers like to know: the impelling motives to action; the struggle in the face of opposition; the vexation under ridicule; and the despair in success too long deferred. Moreover, there is an interest in history written from a subjective point of view that may compensate the reader in this case for any seeming egotism or partiality he may discover. As an autobiography is more interesting than a sketch by another, so is a history written by its actors, as in both cases we get nearer the soul of the subject.

We have finished our task, and we hope the contribution we have made may enable some other hand in the future to write a more complete history of 'the most momentous reform that has yet been launched on the world – the first organised protest against the injustice which has brooded over the character and destiny of one half the human race.'*

AN INTRODUCTION TO

WOMEN'S SUFFRAGE

THE PROLONGED SLAVERY of woman is the darkest page in human history. A survey of the condition of the race through those barbarous periods when physical force governed the world, when the motto 'might makes right' was the law, enables one to account for the origin of woman's subjection to man without referring the fact to the general inferiority of the sex, or Nature's law.

Writers on this question differ as to the cause of the universal degradation of woman in all periods and nations.

One of the greatest minds of the century has thrown a ray of light on this gloomy picture by tracing the origin of woman's slavery to the same principle of selfishness and love of power in man that has thus far dominated all weaker nations and classes. This brings hope of final emancipation, for as all nations and classes are gradually, one after another, asserting and maintaining their independence, the path is clear for woman to follow.

The slavish instinct of an oppressed class has led her to toil patiently through the ages, giving all and asking little, cheerfully sharing with man all perils and privations by land and sea, that husband and sons might attain honour and success. Justice and freedom for herself is her latest and highest demand.

Another writer asserts that the tyranny of man over woman has its roots, after all, in his nobler feelings – his love, his chivalry and his desire to protect woman in the barbarous periods of pillage, lust and war. But wherever the roots may be traced, the results at this hour are equally disastrous to woman. Her best interests and happiness do not seem to have been consulted in the arrangements made for her protection. She has been bought and sold, caressed and crucified at the will and pleasure of her master. But if a chivalrous desire to protect woman has always been the mainspring of man's dominion over her, it should have prompted him to place in her hands the same weapons of defence he has found to be most effective against wrong and oppression.

It is often asserted that as woman has always been man's slave – subject, inferior, dependent, under all forms of government and religion – slavery must be her normal condition. This might have some weight had not the vast majority of men also been enslaved for centuries to kings and popes and orders of nobility, who, in the progress of civilisation, have reached complete equality. And did we not also see the great changes in woman's condition, the marvellous transformation in her character, from a toy in the Turkish harem or a drudge in the German fields to a leader of thought in the literary circles of France, England and America!

In an age when the wrongs of society are adjusted in the courts and at the ballot box, material force yields to reason and majorities.

Woman's steady march onward, and her growing desire for a broader outlook, prove that she has not reached her normal condition, and that society has not yet conceded all that is necessary for its attainment.

Moreover, woman's discontent increases in exact proportion to her development. Instead of a feeling of gratitude for rights accorded, the wisest are indignant at the assumption of any legal disability based on sex, and their feelings in this matter are a surer test of what her nature demands than the feelings and prejudices of the sex claiming to be superior. American men may quiet their consciences with the delusion that no such injustice exists in this country as in Eastern nations, though, with the general improvement in our institutions, woman's condition must inevitably have improved also, yet the same principle that degrades her in Turkey insults her in this republic. Custom forbids a woman there to enter a mosque, or call the hour for prayers; here it forbids her a voice in Church councils or State legislatures. The same taint of her primitive state of slavery affects both latitudes.

The condition of married women, under the laws of all countries, has been essentially that of slaves, until modified, in some respects, within the last quarter of a century in the United States. The change from the old common law of England, in regard to the civil rights of women, from 1848 to the advance legislation in most of the northern states in 1880, marks an era both in the status of woman as a citizen and in our American system of jurisprudence. When the State of New York gave married women certain rights of property,* the individual existence of the wife was recognised, and the old idea that 'husband and wife are one, and that one the husband'* received its death blow. From that hour the statutes of the several states have been steadily diverging from the old English codes. Most of the western states copied the advance legislation of New York, and some are now even more liberal.

The broader demand for political rights has not commanded the thought its merits and dignity should have secured. While complaining of many wrongs and oppressions, women themselves did not see that the political disability of sex was the cause of all their special grievances, and that to secure equality anywhere, it must be recognised everywhere. Like all disfranchised classes, they began by asking to have certain wrongs redressed, and not by asserting their own right to make laws for themselves.

Overburdened with cares in the isolated home, women had not the time, education, opportunity and pecuniary independence to put their thoughts clearly and concisely into propositions, nor the courage to compare their opinions with one another, nor to publish them to any great extent to the world.

It requires philosophy and heroism to rise above the opinion of the wise men of all nations and races, that to be unknown is the highest testimonial woman can have to her virtue, delicacy and refinement.

A certain odium has ever rested on those who have risen above the conventional level and sought new spheres for thought and action, and especially on the few who demand complete equality in political rights. The leaders in this movement have been women of superior mental and physical organisation, of good social standing and education, remarkable alike for their domestic virtues, knowledge of public affairs and rare executive ability, good speakers and writers, inspiring and conducting the genuine reforms of the day, everywhere exerting themselves to promote the best interests of society; yet they have been uniformly ridiculed, misrepresented and denounced in public and private by all classes of society.

Woman's political equality with man is the legitimate outgrowth of the fundamental principles of our Government, clearly set forth in the Declaration of Independence in 1776, in the United States Constitution, adopted in 1784, in the prolonged debates on the origin of human rights in the anti-slavery conflict in 1840, and in the more recent discussions of the party in power since 1865,* on the thirteenth, fourteenth and fifteenth amendments to the national Constitution;* and the majority of our leading statesmen have taken the ground that suffrage is a natural right that may be regulated, but can not be abolished by state law.

21

Under the influence of these liberal principles of republicanism that pervades all classes of American minds, however vaguely, if suddenly called out, they might be stated: woman readily perceives the anomalous position she occupies in a republic, where the Government and religion alike are based on individual conscience and judgement – where the natural rights of all citizens have been exhaustively discussed, and repeatedly declared equal.

From the inauguration of the Government, representative women have expostulated against the inconsistencies between our principles and practices as a nation. Beginning with special grievances, woman's protests soon took a larger scope. Having petitioned state legislatures to change the statutes that robbed her of children, wages and property, she demanded that the constitutions – state and national – be so amended as to give her a voice in the laws, a choice in the rulers and protection in the exercise of her rights as a citizen of the United States.

While the laws affecting woman's civil rights have been greatly improved during the past thirty years, the political demand has made but a questionable progress, though it must be counted as the chief influence in modifying the laws. The selfishness of man was readily enlisted in securing woman's civil rights, while the same element in his character antagonised her demand for political equality.

Fathers who had estates to bequeath to their daughters could see the advantage of securing to woman certain property rights that might limit the legal power of profligate husbands.

Husbands in extensive business operations could see the advantage of allowing the wife the right to hold separate property, settled on her in times of prosperity, that might not be seized for his debts. Hence in the several states able men championed these early measures. But political rights, involving in their last results equality everywhere, roused all the antagonism of a dominant power against the self-assertion of a class hitherto subservient. Men saw that, with political equality for woman, they could no longer keep her in social subordination, and 'the majority of the male sex', says John Stuart Mill, 'can not yet tolerate the idea of living with an equal.'* The fear of a social revolution thus complicated the discussion. The Church, too, took alarm, knowing that with the freedom and education acquired in becoming a component part of the Government, woman would not only outgrow the power of the priesthood and religious superstitions, but would also invade the pulpit, interpret the Bible anew from her own standpoint and claim an equal voice in all ecclesiastical councils. With fierce warnings and denunciations from the pulpit, and false interpretations of scripture, women have been intimidated and misled, and their religious feelings have been played upon for their more complete subjugation. While the general principles of the Bible are in favour of the most enlarged freedom and equality of the race, isolated texts have been used to block the wheels of progress in all periods; thus bigots have defended capital punishment, intemperance, slavery, polygamy and the subjection of woman. The creeds of all nations make obedience to man the cornerstone of her religious character. Fortunately, however, more liberal minds are now giving us higher and purer expositions of the scriptures.

As the social and religious objections appeared against the demand for political rights, the discussion became many-sided, contradictory and as varied as the idiosyncrasies of individual character. Some said, 'Man is woman's natural protector, and she can safely trust him to make laws for her.' She might with fairness reply, as he uniformly robbed her of all property rights to 1848, 'He can not safely be trusted with her personal rights in 1880, though the fact that he did make some restitution at last might modify her distrust in the future.' However, the calendars of our courts still show that fathers deal unjustly with daughters, husbands with wives, brothers with sisters and sons with their own mothers. Though woman needs the protection of one man against his whole sex, in pioneer life, in threading her way through a lonely forest, on the highway or in the streets of the metropolis on a dark night, she sometimes needs, too, the protection of all men against this one. But even if she could be sure, as she is not, of the ever-present, all-protecting power of one strong arm, that would be weak indeed compared with the subtle, all-pervading influence of just and equal laws for all women. Hence woman's need of the ballot, that she may hold in her own right hand the weapon of self-protection and self-defence.

Again it is said: 'The women who make the demand are few in number, and their feelings and opinions are abnormal, and therefore of no weight in considering the aggregate judgement on the question.' The number is larger than appears on the surface, for the fear of public ridicule and the loss of private favours from those who shelter, feed and clothe them withhold many from declaring their opinions and demanding their rights. The ignorance and indifference of the majority of women as to their status as citizens of a republic is not remarkable, for history shows that the masses of all oppressed classes, in the most degraded conditions, have been stolid and apathetic until partial success had crowned the faith and enthusiasm of the few.

The insurrections on Southern plantations were always defeated by the doubt and duplicity of the slaves themselves. That little band of heroes who precipitated the American Revolution in 1776* were so ostracised that they walked the streets with bowed heads, from a sense of loneliness and apprehension. Woman's apathy to the wrongs of her sex, instead of being a plea for her remaining in her present condition, is the strongest argument against it. How completely demoralised by her subjection must she be who does not feel her personal dignity assailed when all women are ranked in every state constitution with idiots, lunatics, criminals and minors;* when in the name of Justice man holds one scale for woman, another for himself; when by the spirit and letter of the laws she is made responsible for crimes committed against her, while the male criminal goes free;* when from altars where she worships no woman may preach; when in the courts, where girls of tender age may be arraigned for the crime of infanticide, she may not plead for the most miserable of her sex; when colleges she is taxed to build and endow deny her the right to share in their advantages;* when she finds that which should be her glory — her possible motherhood — treated everywhere by man as a disability and a crime! A woman insensible to such indignities needs some transformation into nobler thought, some purer atmosphere to breathe, some higher standpoint from which to study human rights.

It is said, 'The difference between the sexes indicates different spheres.' It would be nearer the truth to say the difference indicates different duties in the same sphere, seeing that man and woman were evidently made for each other, and have shown equal capacity in the ordinary range of human duties. In governing nations, leading armies, piloting ships across the sea, rowing lifeboats in terrific gales, in art, science, invention, literature, woman has proved herself the complement of man in the world of thought and action. This difference does not compel us to spread our tables with different food for man and woman, nor to provide in our common schools a different course of study for boys and girls. Sex pervades all nature, yet the male and female tree and vine and shrub rejoice in the same sunshine and shade. The earth and air are free to all the fruits and flowers, yet each absorbs what best ensures its growth. But whatever it is, it requires no special watchfulness on our part to see that it is maintained. This plea, when closely analysed, is generally found to mean woman's inferiority.

The superiority of man, however, does not enter into the demand for suffrage, for in this country all men vote; and as the lower orders of men are not superior, either by nature or grace, to the higher orders of women, they must hold and exercise the right of self-government on some other ground than superiority to women.

Again it is said, 'Woman when independent and self-asserting will lose her influence over man.' In the happiest conditions in life, men and women will ever be mutually dependent on each other. The complete development of all woman's powers will not make her less capable of steadfast love and friendship, but give her new strength to meet the emergencies of life, to aid those who look to her for counsel and support. Men are uniformly more attentive to women of rank, family and fortune, who least need their care, than to any other class. We do not see their protecting love generally extending to the helpless and unfortunate ones of earth. Wherever the skilled hands and cultured brain of woman have made the battle of life easier for man, he has readily pardoned her sound judgement and proper self-assertion. But the prejudices and preferences of man should be a secondary consideration in presence of the individual happiness and freedom of woman. The formation of her character and its influence on the human race is a larger question than man's personal liking. There is no fear, however, that when a superior order of women shall grace the earth there will not be an order of men to match them, and influence over such minds will atone for the loss of it elsewhere.

An honest fear is sometimes expressed, 'that woman would degrade politics, and politics would degrade woman.' As the influence of woman has been uniformly elevating in new civilisations, in missionary work in heathen nations, in schools, colleges, literature and in general society, it is fair to suppose that politics would prove no exception. On the other hand, as the art of government is the most exalted of all sciences, and statesmanship requires the highest order of mind, the ennobling and refining influence of such pursuits must elevate rather than degrade woman. When politics degenerate into bitter persecutions and vulgar court-gossip, they are degrading to man, and his honour, virtue, dignity and refinement are as valuable to woman as her virtues are to him.

Again, it is said, 'Those who make laws must execute them; government needs force behind it – a woman could not be a sheriff or a policeman.' She might not fill these offices in the way men do, but she might far more effectively guard the morals of society and the sanitary conditions of our cities. It might with equal force be said that a woman of culture and artistic taste can not keep house, because she can not wash and iron with her own hands and clean the range and furnace. At the head of the police, a woman could direct her forces and keep order without ever using a baton or a pistol in her own hands. 'The elements of sovereignty,' says Blackstone, 'are three: wisdom, goodness and power.'* Conceding to woman wisdom and goodness, as they are not strictly masculine virtues, and substituting moral power for physical force, we have the necessary elements of government for most of life's emergencies. Women manage families, mixed schools, charitable institutions, large boarding houses and hotels, farms and steam engines, drunken and disorderly men and women, and stop street fights as well as men do. The queens in history compare favourably with the kings.

But, 'In the settlement of national difficulties,' it is said, 'the last resort is war; shall we summon our wives and mothers to the battlefield?' Women have led armies in all ages, have held positions in the army and navy for years in disguise. Some fought, bled and died on the battlefield in our late war.* They performed severe labours in the hospitals and sanitary department. Wisdom would dictate a division of labour in war as well as in peace, assigning each their appropriate department.

Numerous classes of men who enjoy their political rights are exempt from military duty. All men over forty-five, all who suffer mental or physical disability, such as the loss of an eye or a forefinger, clergymen, physicians, Quakers, schoolteachers, professors and presidents of colleges, judges, legislators, congressmen, state prison officials and all county, state and national officers, fathers, brothers or sons having certain relatives dependent on them for support... all of these summed up in every state in the union make millions of voters thus exempted.

In view of this fact, there is no force in the plea that, 'If women vote they must fight.' Moreover, war is not the normal state of the human family in its higher development, but merely a feature of barbarism lasting on through the transition of the race, from the savage to the scholar. When England and America settled the *Alabama* Claims by the Geneva Arbitration,* they pointed the way for the future adjustment of all national difficulties.

Some fear, 'If women assume all the duties political equality implies, the time and attention necessary to the duties of home life will be absorbed in the affairs of state.' The act of voting occupies but little time in itself, and the vast majority of women will attend to their family and social affairs to the neglect of the state, just as men do to their individual interests. The virtue of patriotism is subordinate in most souls to individual and family aggrandisement. As to offices, it is not to be supposed that the class of men now elected will resign to women their chances, and if they should to any extent, the necessary number of women to fill the offices would make no apparent change in our social circles. If, for example, the Senate of the United States should be entirely composed of women, but two in each state would be withdrawn from the pursuit of domestic happiness. For many reasons, under all circumstances, a comparatively smaller proportion of women than men would actively engage in politics.

As the power to extend or limit the suffrage rests now wholly in the hands of man, he can commence the experiment with as small a number as he sees fit, by requiring any lawful qualification. Men were admitted on property and educational qualifications in most of the states at one time – and still are in some – so hard has it been for man to understand the theory of self-government. Three fourths of the women would be thus disqualified, and the remaining fourth would be too small a minority to precipitate a social revolution or defeat masculine measures in the halls of legislation, even if women were a unit on all questions and invariably voted together, which they would not. In this view, the path of duty is plain for the prompt action of those gentlemen who fear universal suffrage for women but are willing to grant it on property and educational qualifications. While those who are governed by the law of expediency should give the measure of justice they deem safe, let those who trust the absolute right proclaim the higher principle in government: 'Equal rights to all.'

Many seeming obstacles in the way of woman's enfranchisement will be surmounted by reforms in many directions. Co-operative labour and co-operative homes will remove many difficulties in the way of woman's success as artisan and housekeeper, when admitted to the governing power. The varied forms of progress, like parallel lines, move forward simultaneously in the same direction. Each reform at its inception seems out of joint with all its surroundings, but the discussion changes the conditions, and brings them in line with the new idea.

The isolated household is responsible for a large share of woman's ignorance and degradation. A mind always in contact with children and servants, whose aspirations and ambitions rise no higher than the roof that shelters it, is necessarily dwarfed in its proportions. The advantages to the few whose fortunes enable them to make the isolated household a more successful experiment can not outweigh the difficulties of the many who are wholly sacrificed to its maintenance.

Quite as many false ideas prevail as to woman's true position in the home as to her status elsewhere. Womanhood is the great fact in her life; wifehood and motherhood are but incidental relations. Governments legislate for men; we do not have one code for bachelors, another for husbands and fathers; neither have the social relations of women any significance in their demands for civil and political rights. Custom and philosophy, in regard to woman's happiness, are alike based on the idea that her strongest social sentiment is love of children; that in this relation her soul finds complete satisfaction. But the love of offspring, common to all orders of women and all forms of animal life, tender and beautiful as it is, can not as a sentiment rank with conjugal love. The one calls out only the negative virtues that belong to apathetic classes, such as patience, endurance, self-sacrifice, exhausting the brain forces, ever giving, asking nothing in return; the other, the outgrowth of the two supreme powers in nature, the positive and negative magnetism, the centrifugal and centripetal forces, the masculine and feminine elements, possessing the divine power of creation, in the universe of thought and action. Two pure souls fused into one by an impassioned love – friends, counsellors, a mutual support and inspiration to each other amid life's struggles – must know the highest human happiness; this is marriage; and this is the only cornerstone of an enduring home. Neither does ordinary motherhood, assumed without any high purpose or preparation, compare in sentiment with the lofty ambition and conscientious devotion of the artist whose pure children of the brain in poetry, painting, music and science are ever beckoning her upwards into an ideal world of beauty. They who give the world a true philosophy, a grand poem, a beautiful painting or statue, or can tell the story of every wandering star – a George Eliot, a Rosa Bonheur, an Elizabeth Barrett Browning, a Maria Mitchell,* whose blood has flowed to the higher arches of the brain – have lived to a holier purpose than they whose children are of the flesh alone, into whose minds they have breathed no clear perceptions of great principles, no moral aspiration, no spiritual life.

Her rights are as completely ignored in what is adjudged to be woman's sphere as out of it; the woman is uniformly sacrificed to the wife and mother. Neither law, gospel, public sentiment nor domestic affection shield her from excessive and enforced maternity, depleting alike to mother and child; all opportunity for mental improvement, health, happiness – yea, life itself – being ruthlessly sacrificed. The wizened, weary, withered, narrow-minded wife – mother of half a dozen children – her interests all centring at her fireside, forms a painful contrast in many a household to the liberal, genial, brilliant, cultured husband in the zenith of his power, who has never given one thought to the higher life, liberty and happiness of the woman by his side, believing her self-abnegation to be Nature's law.

It is often asked if political equality would not rouse antagonisms between the sexes. If it could be proved that men and women had been harmonious in all ages and countries, and that women were happy and satisfied in their slavery, one might hesitate in proposing any change whatever. But the apathy, the helpless, hopeless resignation of a subjected class, can not be called happiness. The more complete the despotism, the more smoothly all things move on the surface. 'Order reigns in Warsaw.'* In the right conditions, the interests of man and woman are essentially one, but in false conditions they must ever be opposed. The principle of equality of rights underlies all human sentiments, and its assertion by any individual or class must rouse antagonism, unless conceded. This has been the battle of the ages, and will be until all forms of slavery are banished from the earth. Philosophers, historians, poets, novelists alike paint woman the victim ever of man's power and selfishness. And now all writers on Eastern civilisation tell us the one insurmountable obstacle to the improvement of society in those countries is the ignorance and superstition of the women. Stronger than the trammels of custom and law is her religion, which teaches that her condition is Heaven-ordained. As the most ignorant minds cling with the greatest tenacity to the dogmas and traditions of their faith, a reform that involves an attack on that stronghold can only be carried by the education of another generation. Hence the self-assertion, the antagonism, the rebellion of woman, so much deplored in England and the United States, is the hope of our higher civilisation. A woman growing up under American ideas of liberty in government and religion, having never blushed behind a Turkish mask, nor pressed her feet in Chinese shoes, can not brook any disabilities based on sex alone without a deep feeling of antagonism with the power that creates it. The change needed to restore good feeling can not be reached by remanding woman to the spinning wheel and the contentment of her grandmother, but by conceding to her every right which the spirit of the age demands. Modern inventions have banished the spinning wheel, and the same law of progress makes the woman of today a different woman from her grandmother.

With these brief replies to the oft-repeated objections made by the opposition we hope to rouse new thoughts in minds prepared to receive them. That equal rights for woman have not long ago been secured is due to causes beyond the control of the actors in this reform. 'The success of a movement,' says Lecky, 'depends much less upon the force of its arguments, or upon the ability of its advocates, than the predisposition of society to receive it.'*

PRECEDING CAUSES

A S CIVILISATION ADVANCES there is a continual change in the standard of human rights. In barbarous ages the right of the strongest was the only one recognised; but as mankind progressed in the arts and sciences intellect began to triumph over brute force. Change is a law of life, and the development of society a natural growth. Although to this law we owe the discoveries of unknown worlds, the inventions of machinery, swifter modes of travel and clearer ideas as to the value of human life and thought, yet each successive change has met with the most determined opposition. Fortunately, progress is not the result of pre-arranged plans of individuals, but is born of a fortuitous combination of circumstances that compel certain results, overcoming the natural inertia of mankind. There is a certain enjoyment in habitual sluggishness, in rising each morning with the same ideas as the night before, in retiring each night with the thoughts of the morning. This inertia of mind and body has ever held the multitude in chains. Thousands have thus surrendered their most sacred rights of conscience. In all periods of human development, thinking has been punished as a crime, which is reason sufficient to account for the general passive resignation of the masses to their conditions and environments.

Again, 'subjection to the powers that be' has been the lesson of both Church and State, throttling science, checking invention, crushing free thought, persecuting and torturing those who have dared to speak or act outside of established authority. Anathemas and the stake have upheld the Church, banishment and the scaffold the throne, and the freedom of mankind has ever been sacrificed to the idea of protection. So entirely has the human will been enslaved in all classes of society in the past that monarchs have humbled themselves to popes, nations have knelt at the feet of monarchs and individuals have sold themselves to others under the subtle promise of 'protection' – a word that simply means release from all responsibility, all use of one's own faculties – a word that has ever blinded people to its true significance. Under authority and this false promise of 'protection', self-reliance, the first incentive to freedom, has not only been lost, but the aversion of mankind for responsibility has been fostered by the few whose greater bodily strength, superior intellect or the inherent law of self-development has impelled to active exertion. Obedience and self-sacrifice – the virtues prescribed for subordinate classes, and which naturally grow out of their condition – are alike opposed to the theory of individual rights and self-government. But as even the inertia of mankind is not proof against the internal law of progress, certain beliefs have been inculcated, certain crimes invented, in order to intimidate the masses. Hence the Church made free thought the worst of sins and the spirit of inquiry the worst of blasphemies, while the State proclaimed her temporal power of divine origin, and all rebellion high treason alike to God and the king, to be speedily and severely punished. In this union of Church and State mankind touched the lowest depth of degradation. As late as the time of Bunyan* the chief doctrine inculcated from the pulpit was obedience to the temporal power.

All these influences fell with crushing weight on woman; more sensitive, helpless and imaginative, she suffered a thousand fears and wrongs where man did one. Lecky, in his *History of Rationalism in Europe*,* shows that the vast majority of the victims of fanaticism and witchcraft, burned, drowned and tortured, were women. Guizot, in his *History of Civilisation*,* while decrying the influence of caste in India, and deploring it as the result of barbarism, thanks God there is no system of caste in Europe – ignoring the fact that, in all its dire and baneful effects, the caste of sex everywhere exists, creating diverse codes of morals for men and women, diverse penalties for crime, diverse industries, diverse religions and educational rights, and diverse relations to the Government. Men are the Brahmans, women the Pariahs* under our existing civilisation. Herbert Spencer's *Descriptive Sociology of England*,* an epitome of English history, says: 'Our laws are based on the all-sufficiency of man's rights, and society exists today for woman only in so far as she is in the keeping of some man.' Thus society, including our systems of jurisprudence, civil and political theories, trade, commerce, education, religion, friendships and family life, has all been framed on the sole idea of man's rights. Hence, he takes upon himself the responsibility of directing and controlling the powers of woman, under that all-sufficient excuse of tyranny, 'divine right'. This same cry of divine authority created the castes of India; has for ages separated its people into bodies with different industrial, educational, civil, religious and political rights; has maintained this separation for the benefit of the superior class, and sedulously taught the doctrine that any change in existing conditions would be a sin of most direful magnitude.

The opposition of theologians, though first to be exhibited when any change is proposed, for reason that change not only takes power from them, but lessens the reverence of mankind for them, is not in its final result so much to be feared as the opposition of those holding political power. The Church, knowing this, has in all ages aimed to connect itself with the State. Political freedom guarantees religious liberty, freedom to worship God according to the dictates of one's own conscience, fosters a spirit of inquiry, creates self-reliance, induces a feeling of responsibility.

The people who demand authority for every thought and action, who look to others for wisdom and protection, are those who perpetuate tyranny. The thinkers and actors who find their authority within are those who inaugurate freedom. Obedience to outside authority to which woman has everywhere been trained has not only dwarfed her capacity, but made her a retarding force in civilisation, recognised at last by statesmen as a dangerous element to free institutions. A recent writer, speaking of Turkey, says: 'All attempts for the improvement of that nation must prove futile, owing to the degradation of its women; and their elevation is hopeless, so long as they are taught by their religion that their condition is ordained of Heaven.'* Gladstone, in one of his pamphlets on the revival of Catholicism in England, says: 'The spread of this religion is due, as might be expected, to woman;'* thus conceding in both cases her power to block the wheels of progress. Hence, in the scientific education of woman, in the training of her faculties to independent thought and logical reasoning, lies the hope of the future.

The two great sources of progress are intellect and wealth. Both represent power, and are the elements of success in life. Education frees the mind from the bondage of authority and makes the individual self-asserting. Remunerative industry is the means of securing to its possessor wealth and education, transforming the labourer to the capitalist. Work in itself is not power; it is but the means to an end. The slave is not benefited by his industry; he does not receive the results of his toil; his labour enriches another – adds to the power of his master to bind his chains still closer. Although woman has performed much of the labour of the world, her industry and economy have been the very means of increasing her degradation. Not being free, the results of her labour have gone to build up and sustain

41

the very class that has perpetuated this injustice. Even in the family, where we should naturally look for the truest conditions, woman has always been robbed of the fruits of her own toil. The influence the Catholic Church has had on religious free thought, that monarchies have had on political free thought, that serfdom has had upon free labour, have all been cumulative in the family upon woman. Taught that father and husband stood to her in the place of God, she has been denied liberty of conscience and held in obedience to masculine will. Taught that the fruits of her industry belonged to others, she has seen man enter into every avocation most suitable to her, while she, the uncomplaining drudge of the household, condemned to the severest labour, has been systematically robbed of her earnings, which have gone to build up her master's power, and she has found herself in the condition of the slave, deprived of the results of her own labour. Taught that education for her was indelicate and irreligious, she has been kept in such gross ignorance as to fall a prey to superstition, and to glory in her own degradation. Taught that a low voice is an excellent thing in woman, she has been trained to a subjugation of the vocal organs, and thus lost the benefit of loud tones and their well-known invigoration of the system. Forbidden to run, climb or jump, her muscles have been weakened, and her strength deteriorated. Confined most of the time to the house, she has neither as strong lungs nor as vigorous a digestion as her brother. Forbidden to enter the pulpit, she has been trained to an unquestioning reverence for theological authority and false belief upon the most vital interests of religion. Forbidden the medical profession, she has at the most sacred times of her life been left to the ignorant supervision of male physicians, and seen her young children die by thousands. Forbidden to enter the courts, she has seen her sex unjustly tried and condemned for crimes men were incapable of judging.

Woman has been the great unpaid labourer of the world, and although within the last two decades a vast number of new employments have been opened to her, statistics prove that in the great majority of these she is not paid according to the value of the work done, but according to sex. The opening of all industries to woman, and the wage question as connected with her, are most subtle and profound questions of political economy, closely interwoven with the rights of self-government.

The revival of learning had its influence upon woman, and we find in the early part of the fourteenth century a decided tendency towards a recognition of her equality. Christine of Pisa,* the most eminent woman of this period, supported a family of six persons by her pen, taking high ground on the conservation of morals in opposition to the general licentious spirit of the age. Margaret of Angoulême, the brilliant Queen of Navarre, was a voluminous writer, her *Heptaméron* rising to the dignity of a French classic.* A paper in the *Revue des Deux Mondes** a few years since, by M. Henri Baudrillart, upon the 'Emancipation of Woman',* recalls the fact that for nearly four hundred years, men, too, have been ardent believers in equal rights for woman.

In 1509, Cornelius Agrippa, a great literary authority of his time, published a work of this character. Agrippa was not content with claiming woman's equality, but in a work of thirty chapters devoted himself to proving 'the superiority of woman'.* In less than fifty years (1552) Ruscelli* brought out a similar work based on the Platonic philosophy. In 1599, Anthony Gibson wrote a book which in the prolix phraseology of the times was called *A Woman's Worth, Defended Against All the Men in the World, Proving Them to Be More Perfect, Excellent and Absolute, in All Virtuous Actions, than any Man of what Quality Soever.** While these sturdy male defenders of the rights of woman met with many opponents, some going so far as to assert that women were beings not endowed with reason, they were sustained by many vigorous writers among women. Italy, then the foremost literary country of Europe, possessed many women of learning, one of whom, Lucrezia Morinella, a Venetian lady, wrote a work entitled *The Nobleness and Excellence of Women, Together with the Faults and Imperfections of Men.**

The seventeenth century gave birth to many essays and books of a like character, not confined to the laity, as several friars wrote upon the same subject. In 1696, Daniel Defoe wished to have an institute founded for the better education of young women. He said: 'We reproach the sex every day for folly and impertinence, while I am confident had they the advantages of education equal to us, they would be guilty of less than ourselves.'* Alexander's *History of Women*, John Paul Ribera's work upon women, the two huge quartos of De Costa upon the same subject,

Count Ségur's *Women: Their Condition and Influence* and many other works showed the drift of the new age.*

The Reformation, that great revolution in religious thought, loosened the grasp of the Church upon woman, and is to be looked upon as one of the most important steps in this reform. In the reign of Elizabeth, England was called the Paradise of Women. When Elizabeth ascended the throne, it was not only as queen, but she succeeded her father as the head of the newly formed rebellious Church, and she held firm grasp on both Church and State during the long years of her reign, bending alike priest and prelate to her fiery will. The reign of Queen Anne, called the Golden Age of English Literature, is especially noticeable on account of Mary Astell and Elizabeth Elstob.* The latter, speaking nine languages, was most famous for her skill in the Saxon tongue. She also replied to current objections made to woman's learning. Mary Astell elaborated a plan for a woman's college, which was favourably received by Queen Anne, and would have been carried out, but for the opposition of Bishop Burnett.*

During the latter part of the eighteenth century, there were public discussions by women in England, under the general head of Female Parliament. These discussions took wide range, touching upon the entrance of men into those industries usually assigned to women, and demanding for themselves higher educational advantages, and the right to vote at elections, and to be returned members of Parliament.

The American Revolution, that great political rebellion of the ages, was based upon the inherent rights of the individual. Perhaps in none but English colonies, by descendants of English parents, could such a revolution have been consummated. England had never felt the bonds of feudalism to the extent of many countries; its people had defied its monarchs and wrested from them many civil rights – rights which protected women as well as men – and although its common law, warped by ecclesiasticism, expended its chief rigors upon women, yet at an early day they enjoyed certain ecclesiastical and political powers unknown to women elsewhere. Before the Conquest,* abbesses sat in councils of the Church and signed its decrees, while kings were even dependent upon their consent in granting certain charters. The synod of Whitby, in the ninth century, was held in the convent of the Abbess Hilda,* she herself presiding over its deliberations. The famous prophetess of Kent at one period communicated the orders of Heaven to the Pope himself.* Ladies of birth and quality sat in council with the Saxon *witas* – i.e. wise men – taking part in the Witenaġemot, the great National Council of our Saxon ancestors in England.* In the seventh century this National Council met at Baghamstead to enact a new code of laws,* the queen, abbesses and many ladies of quality taking part and signing the decrees. Passing by other similar instances, we find in the reign of Henry III that four women took seats in Parliament, and in the reign of Edward I ten ladies were called to Parliament, while in the thirteenth century, Queen Elinor became

Keeper of the Great Seal, sitting as Lord Chancellor in the *Aula Regia*,* the highest court of the Kingdom. Running back two or three centuries before the Christian era, we find Martia,* her seat of power in London, holding the reins of government so wisely as to receive the surname of Proba, the Just. She especially devoted herself to the enactment of just laws for her subjects, the first principles of the common law tracing back to her; the celebrated laws of Alfred and of Edward the Confessor being in great degree restorations and compilations from the laws of Martia, which were known as the Martian Statutes.

When the American colonies began their resistance to English tyranny, the women – all this inherited tendency to freedom surging in their veins – were as active, earnest, determined and self-sacrificing as the men, and although, as Mrs Ellet in her *Women of the Revolution** remarks, 'political history says but little, and that vaguely and incidentally, of the women who bore their part in the revolution,' yet that little shows woman to have been endowed with as lofty a patriotism as man, and to have as fully understood the principles upon which the struggle was based. Among the women who manifested deep political insight were Mercy Otis Warren, Abigail Smith Adams and Hannah Lee Corbin,* all closely related to the foremost men of the Revolution. Mrs Warren was a sister of James Otis, whose fiery words did so much to arouse and intensify the feelings of the colonists against British aggression. This brother and sister were united to the end of their lives in a friendship rendered firm and enduring by the similarity of their intellects and political views. The home of Mrs Warren was the resort of patriotic spirits and the headquarters of the rebellion. She herself wrote, 'By the Plymouth fireside were many political plans organised, discussed and digested.' Her correspondence with eminent men of the Revolution was extensive and belongs to the history of the country. She was the first one who based the struggle upon 'inherent rights', a phrase afterwards made the cornerstone of political authority. Mrs Warren asserted that 'inherent rights' belonged to all mankind, and had been conferred on all by the God of nations. She numbered Jefferson among her correspondents, and the Declaration of Independence shows the influence of her mind. Among others who sought her counsel upon political matters were Samuel and John Adams, Dickinson, that pure patriot of Pennsylvania, Jefferson, Gerry and Knox.* She was the first person who counselled separation* and pressed those views upon John Adams when he sought her advice before the opening of the first Congress. At that time even Washington had no thought of the final independence of the colonies, emphatically denying such intention or desire on their part, and John Adams was shunned in the streets of Philadelphia for having dared to hint such a possibility. Mrs Warren sustained his sinking courage and urged him to bolder steps. Her advice was not only sought in every emergency, but political parties found their arguments in her conversation. Mrs Warren looked not to the freedom of man alone, but to that of her own sex also.

England itself had at least one woman who watched the struggle of America with lively interest, and whose writings aided in the dissemination of republican ideas. This was the celebrated Catharine Sawbridge Macaulay,* one of the greatest minds England has ever produced – a woman so noted for her republican ideas that after her death a statue was erected to her as the 'Patroness of Liberty'. During the whole of the Revolutionary period, Washington was in correspondence with Mrs Macaulay, who did much to sustain him during those days of trial. She and Mrs Warren were also correspondents at that time. She wrote several works of a republican character, for home influence; among these, in 1775, *An Address to the People of England, Scotland and Ireland, on the Present Important Crisis of Affairs*, designed to show the justice of the American cause. The gratitude Americans feel towards Edmund Burke* for his aid might well be extended to Mrs Macaulay.

Abigail Smith Adams, the wife of John Adams, was an American woman whose political insight was worthy of remark. She early protested against the formation of a new government in which woman should be unrecognised, demanding for her a voice and representation. She was the first American woman who threatened rebellion unless the rights of her sex were secured. In March 1776, she wrote to her husband, then in the Continental Congress, 'I long to hear you have declared an independency, and, by the way, in the new code of laws which I suppose it will be necessary for you to make, I desire you would remember the ladies, and be more generous and favourable to them than your ancestors. Do not put such unlimited power into the hands of husbands. Remember, all men would be tyrants if they could. If particular care and attention are not paid to the ladies, we are determined to foment a rebellion, and will not hold ourselves bound to obey any laws in which we have no voice or representation.' Again and again did Mrs Adams urge the establishment of an independency and the limitation of man's power over woman, declaring all arbitrary power dangerous and tending to revolution. Nor was she less mindful of equal advantages of education. 'If you complain of education in sons, what shall I say in regard to daughters, who every day experience the want of it?' She expressed a strong wish that the new Constitution might be distinguished for its encouragement of learning and virtue. Nothing more fully shows the dependent condition of a class than the methods used to secure their wishes. Mrs Adams felt herself obliged to appeal to masculine selfishness in showing the reflex action woman's education would have upon man. 'If,' said she, 'we mean to have heroes, statesmen and philosophers, we should have learned women.' Thus did the Revolutionary Mothers urge the recognition of equal rights when the Government was in the process of formation. Although the first plot of ground in the United States for a public school had been given by a woman (Bridget Grafford*) in 1700, her sex were denied admission. Mrs Adams, as well as her friend Mrs Warren, had in their own persons felt the deprivations of early educational advantages. The boasted public school system of Massachusetts, created for boys only, opened at last its doors to girls, merely to secure its share of public money. The women of the South, too, early demanded political equality. The counties of Mecklenberg and Rowan, North Carolina, were famous for the patriotism of their women. Mecklenberg claims to have issued the first declaration of independence, and, at the centennial celebration of this event in May 1875, proudly accepted for itself the derisive name given this region by Tarleton's* officers, 'The Hornet's Nest of America.' This name – first bestowed by British officers upon Mrs Brevard's mansion, then Tarleton's headquarters, where that lady's fiery patriotism and stinging wit discomfited this General in many a sally – was at last held to include the whole county. In 1778, only two years after the Declaration of Independence was adopted,* and while the flames of war were still spreading over the country, Hannah Lee Corbin, of Virginia, the sister of General Richard Henry Lee, wrote him, protesting against the taxation of women unless they were allowed to vote. He replied that 'women were already possessed of that right,' thus recognising the fact of woman's enfranchisement as one of the results of the new government, and it is on record that women in Virginia did at an early day exercise the right of voting. New Jersey also specifically secured this right to women on the 2nd of July 1776 – a right exercised by them for more than a third of a century. Thus our country started into governmental life freighted with the protests of the Revolutionary Mothers against being ruled without their consent. From that hour to the present, women have been continually raising their voices against political tyranny, and demanding for themselves equality of opportunity in every department of life.

In 1790, Mary Wollstonecraft's *Vindication of the Rights of Women*,* published in London, attracted much attention from liberal minds. She examined the position of woman in the light of existing civilisations, and demanded for her the widest opportunities of education, industry, political knowledge and the right of representation. Although her work is filled with maxims of the highest morality and purest wisdom, it called forth such violent abuse that her husband appealed for her from the judgement of her contemporaries to that of mankind.* So exalted were her ideas of woman, so comprehensive her view of life, that Margaret Fuller,* in referring to her, said: 'Mary Wollstonecraft – a woman whose existence proved the need of some new interpretation of woman's rights, belonging to that class who by birth find themselves in places so narrow that, by breaking bonds, they become outlaws.' Following her came Jane Marcet, Eliza Lynn and Harriet Martineau* – each of whom, in the early part of the nineteenth century, exerted a decided influence upon the political thought of England. Mrs Marcet was one of the most scientific and highly cultivated persons of the age. Her *Conversations on Chemistry** familiarised that science both in England and America, and from it various male writers filched their ideas. It was a textbook in this country for many years. Over one hundred and sixty thousand copies were sold, though the fact that this work

emanated from the brain of a woman was carefully with-
held. Mrs Marcet also wrote upon political economy,* and
was the first person who made the subject comprehensive
to the popular mind. Her manner of treating it was so
clear and vivid that the public, to whom it had been a hidden science, were able to grasp the subject. Her writings
were the inspiration of Harriet Martineau, who followed
her in the same department of thought at a later period.
Miss Martineau was a remarkable woman. Besides her
numerous books on political economy, she was a regular
contributor to the London *Daily News*, the second paper
in circulation in England, for many years writing five long
articles weekly, also to Dickens' *Household Words*, and the
Westminster Review.* She saw clearly the spirit and purpose
of the Anti-Slavery Movement in this country, and was
a regular contributor to the *National Anti-Slavery Standard*,*
published in New York. Eliza Lynn, an Irish lady, was at
this time writing leading editorials for political papers.
In Russia, Catharine II,* the absolute and irresponsible
ruler of that vast nation, gave utterance to views of which,
says La Harpe,* the revolutionists of France and America
fondly thought themselves the originators. She caused her
grandchildren to be educated into the most liberal ideas,
and Russia was at one time the only country in Europe
where political refugees could find safety. To Catharine,
Russia is indebted for the first proposition to enfranchise
the serfs, but meeting strong opposition she was obliged to
relinquish this idea, which was carried to fruition by her
great-grandson, Alexander.

53

This period of the eighteenth century was famous for the executions of women on account of their radical political opinions, Madame Roland, the leader of the liberal party in France, going to the guillotine with the now famous words upon her lips, 'Oh, Liberty, what crimes are committed in thy name!' The beautiful Charlotte Corday sealed with her life her belief in liberty, while Sophie Lapierre barely escaped the same fate; though two men, Sieyès and Condorcet, in the midst of the French Revolution, proposed the recognition of woman's political rights.*

Frances Wright,* a person of extraordinary powers of mind, born in Dundee, Scotland, in 1797, was the first woman who gave lectures on political subjects in America. When sixteen years of age she heard of the existence of a country in which freedom for the people had been proclaimed; she was filled with joy and a determination to visit the American Republic, where the foundations of justice, liberty and equality had been so securely laid. In 1820 she came here, travelling extensively north and south. She was at that time but twenty-two years of age.* Her letters gave Europeans the first true knowledge of America, and secured for her the friendship of LaFayette.* Upon her second visit she made this country her home for several years. Her radical ideas on theology, slavery and the social degradation of woman, now generally accepted by the best minds of the age, were then denounced by both press and pulpit, and maintained by her at the risk of her life. Although the Government of the United States was framed on the basis of entire separation of Church and State, yet from an early day the theological spirit had striven to unite the two, in order to strengthen the Church by its union with the civil power. As early as 1828, the standard of the Christian Party in Politics* was openly unfurled. Frances Wright had long been aware of its insidious efforts, and its reliance upon women for its support. Ignorant, superstitious, devout, woman's general lack of education made her a fitting instrument for the work of thus undermining the republic. Having deprived her of her just rights, the country was now to find in woman its most dangerous foe. Frances Wright lectured that winter in the large cities of the west and middle states, striving to rouse the nation to the new danger which threatened it. The clergy at once became her most bitter opponents. The cry of 'infidel' was started on every side, though her work was of vital importance to the country and undertaken from the purest philanthropy. In speaking of her persecutions she said: 'The injury and inconvenience of every kind and every hour to which, in these days, a really consistent reformer stands exposed, none can conceive but those who experience them. Such become, as it were, excommunicated after the fashion of the old Catholic Mother Church, removed even from the protection of law, such as it is, and from the sympathy of society, for whose sake they consent to be crucified.'

Among those who were advocating the higher education of women, Mrs Emma Willard* became noted at this period. Born with a strong desire for learning, she keenly felt the educational disadvantages of her sex. She began teaching at an early day, introducing new studies and new methods in her school, striving to secure public interest in promoting woman's education. Governor Clinton of New York,* impressed with the wisdom of her plans, invited her to move her school from Connecticut to New York. She accepted, and in 1819 established a school in Watervleit, which soon moved to Troy, and in time built up a great reputation. Through the influence of Governor Clinton, the Legislature granted a portion of the educational fund to endow this institution, which was the first instance in the United States of Government aid for the education of women. Amos B. Eaton, Professor of the Natural Sciences in the Rensselaer Institute, Troy, at this time, was Mrs Willard's faithful friend and teacher. In the early days it was her custom, in introducing a new branch of learning into her seminary, to study it herself, reciting to Professor Eaton every evening the lesson of the next day. Thus she went through botany, chemistry, mineralogy, astronomy and the higher mathematics. As she could not afford teachers for these branches, with faithful study she fitted herself. Mrs Willard's was the first girls' school in which the higher mathematics formed part of the course, but such was the prejudice against a liberal education for woman that the first public examination of a girl in geometry (1829) created as bitter a storm of ridicule as has since assailed women who have entered the law, the pulpit or the medical profession. The derision attendant upon the experiment of advancing woman's education led Governor Clinton to say in his message to the Legislature: 'I trust you will not be deterred by commonplace ridicule from extending your munificence to this meritorious institution.' At a school convention in Syracuse, 1845, Mrs Willard suggested the employment of woman as superintendents of public schools, a measure since adopted in many states. She also projected the system of normal schools for the higher education of teachers. A scientific explorer as well as student, she wrote a work on the *Motive Power in the Circulation of the Blood*, in contradiction to Harvey's theory,* which at once attracted the attention of medical men. This work was one of the then accumulating evidences of woman's adaptation to medical study.

In Ancient Egypt the medical profession was in the hands of women, to which we may attribute that country's almost entire exemption from infantile diseases, a fact which recent discoveries fully authenticate. The enormous death rate of young children in modern civilised countries may be traced to woman's general enforced ignorance of the laws of life, and to the fact that the profession of medicine has been too exclusively in the hands of men. Though through the dim past we find women still making discoveries, and in the feudal ages possessing knowledge of both medicine and surgery, it is but recently that they have been welcomed as practitioners into the medical profession. Looking back scarcely a hundred years, we find science much indebted to woman for some of its most brilliant discoveries. In 1736, the first medical botany was given to the world by Elizabeth Blackwell,* a woman physician, whom the persecutions of her male compeers had cast

into jail for debt. As Bunyan prepared his *Pilgrim's Progress**
between prison walls, so did Elizabeth Blackwell, nowise
disheartened, prepare her valuable aid to medical science
under the same conditions. Lady Montague's discovery
of a check to the smallpox, Madam Boivin's discovery of
the hidden cause of certain haemorrhages, Madam du
Coudray's invention of the manikin are among the notable steps which opened the way to the modern Elizabeth
Blackwell, Harriot K. Hunt, Clemence S. Lozier, Ann
Preston, Hannah Longshore, Marie Jackson, Laura Ross
Wolcott, Marie Zakrzewska, and Mary Putnam Jacobi,*
who are some of the earlier distinguished American ex-
amples of woman's skill in the healing art.

Mary Gove Nichols* gave public lectures upon anatomy
in the United States in 1838. Paulina Wright (Davis)*
followed her upon physiology in 1844, using a manikin in
her illustrations.* Mariana Johnson* followed Mrs Davis,
but it was 1848 before Elizabeth Blackwell – the first
woman to pass through the regular course of medical study
– received her diploma at Geneva.* In 1845–46, preceding Miss Blackwell's course of study, Dr Samuel Gregory
and his brother George issued pamphlets advocating the
education and employment of women-physicians, and, in
1847, Dr Gregory delivered a series of lectures in Boston
upon that subject, followed in 1848 by a school numbering twelve ladies, and an association entitled the American Female Medical Education Society.* In 1832, Lydia
Maria Child published her *History of Woman*,* which was
the first American storehouse of information upon the

whole question, and undoubtedly increased the agitation. In 1836, Ernestine L. Rose, a Polish lady – banished from her native country by the Austrian tyrant, Francis Joseph,* for her love of liberty – came to America, lecturing in the large cities north and south upon the 'Science of Government'. She advocated the enfranchisement of woman. Her beauty, wit and eloquence drew crowded houses. About this period Judge Hurlbut of New York, a leading member of the Bar, wrote a vigorous work on *Human Rights*,* in which he advocated political equality for women. This work attracted the attention of many legal minds throughout that state. In the winter of 1836, a bill was introduced into the New York Legislature by Judge Hertell, to secure to married women their rights of property.* This bill was drawn up under the direction of Hon. John Savage, Chief-Justice of the Supreme Court, and Hon. John C. Spencer, one of the revisers of the statutes of New York. It was in furtherance of this bill that Ernestine L. Rose and Paulina Wright* at that early day circulated petitions. The very few names they secured show the hopeless apathy and ignorance of the women as to their own rights. As similar bills* were pending in New York until finally passed in 1848, a great educational work was accomplished in the constant discussion of the topics involved. During the winters of 1844–46, Elizabeth Cady Stanton, living in Albany, made the acquaintance of Judge Hurlbut and a large circle of lawyers and legislators, and, while exerting herself to strengthen their convictions in favour of the pending bill, she resolved at no distant day to call a convention for a full and free discussion of woman's rights and wrongs.

In 1828, Sarah and Angelina Grimké,* daughters of a wealthy planter of Charleston, South Carolina, emancipated their slaves and came north to lecture on the evils of slavery, leaving their home and native place for ever because of their hatred of this wrong. Angelina was a natural orator. Fresh from the land of bondage, there was a fervour in her speech that electrified her hearers and drew crowds wherever she went. Sarah published a book reviewing the Bible arguments the clergy were then making in their pulpits to prove that the degradation of the slave and woman were alike in harmony with the expressed will of God.* Thus women from the beginning took an active part in the anti-slavery struggle. They circulated petitions, raised large sums of money by fairs, held prayer meetings and conventions. In 1835, Angelina wrote an able letter to William Lloyd Garrison, immediately after the Boston mob.* These letters and appeals were considered very effective abolition documents.

In May 1837, a National Woman's Anti-Slavery Convention was held in New York, in which eight states were represented by seventy-one delegates.* The meetings were ably sustained through two days. The different sessions were opened by prayer and reading of the scriptures by the women themselves. A devout, earnest spirit prevailed. The debates, resolutions, speeches and appeals were fully equal to those in any convention held by men of that period. Angelina Grimké was appointed by this convention to prepare an appeal for the slaves to the people of the free states, and a letter to John Quincy Adams thanking him for his services in defending the right of petition for women and slaves, qualified with the regret that, by expressing himself 'adverse to the abolition of slavery in the District of Columbia', he did not sustain the cause of freedom and of God.* She wrote a stirring appeal to the Christian women of the South, urging them to use their influence against slavery. Sarah also wrote an appeal to the clergy of the South, conjuring them to use their power for freedom.

Among those who took part in these conventions we find the names of Lydia Maria Child, Mary Grove, Henrietta Sargent, Sarah Pugh, Abby Kelley, Mary S. Parker of Boston, who was president of the convention, Anne Webster, Deborah Shaw, Martha Storrs, Mrs A.L. Cox, Rebecca B. Spring and Abigail Hopper Gibbons, a daughter of that noble Quaker philanthropist, Isaac T. Hopper.*

Abby Kelley was the most untiring and the most persecuted of all the women who laboured throughout the anti-slavery struggle. She travelled up and down, alike in winter's cold and summer's heat, with scorn, ridicule, violence and mobs accompanying her, suffering all kinds of persecutions, still speaking whenever and wherever she gained an audience – in the open air, in schoolhouse, barn, depot, church or public hall, on weekday or Sunday – as she found opportunity. For listening to her on Sunday many men and women were expelled from their churches. Thus through continued persecution was woman's self-assertion and self-respect sufficiently developed to prompt her at last to demand justice, liberty and equality for herself.

In 1840, Margaret Fuller published an essay in *The Dial*, entitled 'The Great Lawsuit, or Man vs. Woman: Woman vs. Man'.* In this essay she demanded perfect equality for woman, in education, industry and politics. It attracted great attention and was afterwards expanded into a work entitled *Woman in the Nineteenth Century*. This, with her parlour conversations on art, science, religion, politics, philosophy and social life, gave a new impulse to woman's education as a thinker.*

Woman and Her Era by Eliza Woodson Farnham* was another work that called out a general discussion on the status of the sexes, Mrs Farnham taking the ground of woman's superiority. The great social and educational work done by her in California, when society there was chiefly male, and rapidly tending to savagism, and her humane experiment in the Sing Sing (NY) State Prison,* assisted by Georgiana Bruce Kirby and Mariana Johnson,* are worthy of mention.

In the State of New York, in 1845, Revd Samuel J. May* preached a sermon at Syracuse upon 'The Rights and Conditions of Women', in which he sustained their right to take part in political life, saying women need not expect 'to have their wrongs fully redressed until they themselves have a voice and a hand in the enactment and administration of the laws.'

In 1847, Clarina Howard Nichols, in her husband's paper,* addressed to the voters of the State of Vermont a series of editorials, setting forth the injustice of the property disabilities of married women.

In 1849, Lucretia Mott* published a discourse on woman, delivered in the Assembly Building, Philadelphia, in answer to a Lyceum lecture which Richard H. Dana of Boston* was giving in many of the chief cities, ridiculing the idea of political equality for woman. Elizabeth Wilson of Ohio published a scriptural view of woman's rights and duties far in advance of the generally received opinions. At even an earlier day, Martha Bradstreet of Utica* pleaded her own case in the courts of New York, continuing her contest for many years. The temperance reform and the deep interest taken in it by women, the effective appeals they made, setting forth their wrongs as mother, wife, sister and daughter of the drunkard, with a power beyond that of man, early gave them a local place on this platform as a favour, though denied as a right. Delegates from women's societies to state and national conventions invariably found themselves rejected. It was her early labours in the temperance cause that first roused Susan B. Anthony to a realising sense of woman's social, civil and political degradation, and thus secured her lifelong labours for the enfranchisement of woman. In 1847 she made her first speech at a public meeting of the Daughters of Temperance in Canajoharie, NY. The same year Antoinette L. Brown,* then a student at Oberlin College, Ohio, the first institution that made the experiment of co-education,* delivered her first speech on temperance in several places in Ohio, and on women's rights, in the Baptist church at

Henrietta, NY. Lucy Stone,* a graduate of Oberlin, made her first speech on women's rights the same year in her brother's church at Brookfield, Mass.

Nor were the women of Europe inactive during these years. In 1824 Elizabeth Heyrick,* a Quaker woman, cut the Gordian knot of difficulty in the anti-slavery struggle in England, by an able essay in favour of immediate, unconditional emancipation. At Leipzig, in 1844, Helene Marie Weber* – her father a Prussian officer and her mother an English woman – wrote a series of ten tracts on 'Woman's Rights and Wrongs', covering the whole question and making a volume of over twelve hundred pages. The first of these treated of the intellectual faculties; the second, woman's rights of property; the third, wedlock – deprecating the custom of woman merging her civil existence in that of her husband; the fourth claimed woman's right to all political emoluments; the fifth, on ecclesiasticism, demanded for woman an entrance to the pulpit; the sixth, upon suffrage, declared it to be woman's right and duty to vote. These essays were strong, vigorous and convincing. Miss Weber also lectured in Vienna, Berlin and several of the large German cities. In England, Lady Morgan's *Woman and Her Master** appeared – a work filled with philosophical reflections, and of the same general bearing as Miss Weber's. Also an *Appeal of Women*, the joint work of Mrs Wheeler and William Thompson* – a strong and vigorous essay in which woman's limitations under the law were tersely and pungently set forth and her political rights demanded. The active part women took in the

Polish and German revolutions and in favour of the abolition of slavery in the British West Indies all taught their lessons of woman's rights. Madam Mathilde Anneke, on the staff of her husband, with Hon. Carl Schurz, carried messages to and fro in the midst of danger on the battlefields of Germany.*

Thus over the civilised world we find the same impelling forces, and general development of society, without any individual concert of action, tending to the same general result; alike rousing the minds of men and women to the aggregated wrongs of centuries and inciting to an effort for their overthrow.

The works of George Sand, Fredrika Bremer, Charlotte Brontë, George Eliot, Catharine Sedgwick and Harriet Beecher Stowe in literature; Mrs Hemans, Mrs Sigourney, Elizabeth Barrett Browning in poetry; Angelica Kauffman, Rosa Bonheur, Harriet Hosmer in art; Mary Somerville, Caroline Herschel, Maria Mitchell in science; Elizabeth Fry, Dorothea Dix, Mary Carpenter in prison reform; Florence Nightingale and Clara Barton in the camp* are all parts of the great uprising of women out of the lethargy of the past, and are among the forces of the complete revolution a thousand pens and voices herald at this hour.

APPENDIX

On Margaret Fuller

MARGARET FULLER possessed more influence upon the thought of America than any woman previous to her time. Men of diverse interests and habits of thought alike recognised her power and acknowledged the quickening influence of her mind upon their own. Ralph Waldo Emerson* said of her: 'The day was never long enough to exhaust her opulent memory; and I, who knew her intimately for ten years, never saw her without surprise at her new powers.'

William H. Channing, in her memoirs,* says: 'I have no hope of conveying to my readers my sense of the beauty of our relation, as it lies in the past, with brightness falling on it from Margaret's risen spirit. It would be like printing a chapter of autobiography to describe what is so grateful in memory – its influence upon oneself.'

Revd James Freeman Clarke* says: 'Socrates without his scholars would be more complete than Margaret without her friends. The insight which Margaret displayed in finding her friends; the magnetism by which she drew them towards herself; the catholic range of her intimacies; the influence which she exerted to develop the latent germ of every character; the constancy with which she clung to each when she had once given and received confidence; the delicate justice which kept every intimacy separate; and the process of transfiguration which took place when she met anyone on this mountain of friendship, giving a dazzling lustre to the details of common life – all these should be at least touched upon and illustrated to give any adequate view of these relations.' Horace Greeley, in his *Recollections of a Busy Life*,* said: 'When I first made her acquaintance she was mentally the best instructed woman in America.'

When Transcendentalism rose in New England, drawing the brightest minds of the country into its faith, Margaret was accepted as its high priestess; and when *The Dial* was established for the expression of those views, she was chosen its editor, aided by Ralph Waldo Emerson and George Ripley.* Nothing could be more significant of the place Margaret Fuller held in the realm of thought than the fact that in this editorship she was given precedence over the eminent philosopher and eminent scholar, her associates.

She sought to unveil the mysteries of life and enfranchise her own sex from the bondage of the past, and while still under thirty planned a series of conversations (in Boston) for women only, wherein she took a leading part. The general object of these conferences, as declared in her programme, was to supply answers to these questions: 'What are we born to do?' and 'How shall we do it?' or, as has been stated, 'Her three special aims in those conversations were to pass in review the departments of thought and knowledge, and endeavour to place them in one relation to one another in our minds. To systematise thought and give a precision and clearness in which our sex are so deficient, chiefly, I think, because they have so few inducements to test and classify what they receive. To ascertain what pursuits are best suited to us, in our time and state of society, and how we may make the best use of our means of building up the life of thought upon the life of action.'

These conversations continued for several successive winters, and were in reality a vindication of woman's right to think. In calling forth the opinions of her sex upon life, literature, mythology, art, culture and Religion, Miss Fuller was the precursor of the women's rights agitation of the last thirty-three years. Her work 'The Great Lawsuit; or, Man vs. Woman, Woman vs. Man'* was declared by Horace Greeley to be the loftiest and most commanding assertion made of the right of woman to be regarded and treated as an independent, intelligent, rational being, entitled to an equal voice in framing and modifying the laws she is required to obey, and in controlling and disposing of the property she has inherited or aided to acquire. In this work Margaret said: 'It is the fault of marriage and of the present relation between the sexes that the woman *belongs* to the man, instead of forming a whole with him... woman, self-centred, would never be absorbed by any relation; it would only be an experience to her, as to man. It is a vulgar error that love – *a* love – is to woman her whole existence; she is also born for Truth and Love in their universal energy. Would she but assume her inheritance, Mary would not be the only virgin mother.'

Margaret Fuller was the first woman upon the staff of the *New York Tribune*, a position she took in 1844, when she was but thirty-four. Mrs Greeley, having made Margaret's acquaintance, attended her conversations and accepted her leading ideas, planned to have her become a member of the Greeley family and a writer for the *Tribune*; a position was therefore offered her by Mr Greeley upon his wife's judgement. It required but a short time, however, for the great editor to feel her power, although he failed to fully comprehend her greatness. It has been declared not the least of Horace Greeley's services to the nation that he was willing to entrust the literary criticisms of the *Tribune* to one whose standard of culture was so far above that of his readers or his own.

Margaret Fuller opened the way for many women, who upon the editorial staff of the great New York dailies, as literary critics and as reporters, have helped impress woman's thought upon the American mind.

Theodore Parker,* who knew her well, characterised her as a critic, rather than a creator or seer. But whether we look upon her as critic, creator or seer, she was thoroughly a woman. One of her friends wrote of her, 'She was the largest woman, and not a woman who wanted to be a man.' Woman everywhere, today, is a critic. Enthralled as she has been for ages by both religious and political despotism, no sooner does she rouse to thought than she necessarily begins criticism. The hoary wrongs of the past still fall with heavy weight upon woman – their curse still exists. Before building society anew, she seeks to destroy the errors and injustice of the past, hence we find women critics in every department of thought.

PROGRESS OF

THE WOMEN'S MOVEMENT

In the United Kingdom

1900–20*

I CONSIDER IT AN HONOUR to have been asked to take up the pen from the date 1900, when my dear friend and colleague, the late Helen Blackburn,* laid it down after writing the chapter on Great Britain for Volume IV of the *History of Woman Suffrage*. I am particularly fortunate in that it falls to my lot to include the year 1918, when victory crowned our fifty years' struggle in these islands to obtain the Parliamentary franchise for women.*

Several circumstances entirely outside our power of control combined to promote the rapid growth of the movement at the beginning of the twentieth century. The chief of these were the South African war, 1899–1902,* and the death of Queen Victoria in 1901. The war with the Transvaal was caused by the refusal of President Kruger* and his advisers to recognise the principle that taxation and representation should go together. The so-called uitlanders,* who formed a large proportion of the population of the Transvaal and provided by taxation a still larger proportion of its revenue, were practically excluded from representation. This led to intense irritation, and ultimately to war. It was, therefore, inevitable that articles in the press and the speeches of British statesmen dealing with the war used arguments which might have been transferred without the alteration of a single word to women's suffrage speeches.

I have described on pages 29 and 30 of *Women's Suffrage: A Short History of a Great Movement** the strong impulse which had been given to the electoral activity of British women by the Corrupt Practices Act of 1883, which made paid canvassing illegal and otherwise reduced electoral expenses. Very soon after it came into operation both the chief political parties organised bands of educated women to act as canvassers, election agents, etc. in contested elections. The war stimulated this electoral activity of women. A general election was held in 1900, and in the absence of husbands, sons and brothers in South Africa, many wives, mothers and sisters ran the whole election on their behalf. Several of these were well known anti-suffragists. Even Mrs Humphry Ward* herself, on the occasion of an important anti-suffrage meeting in London, excused her absence on the grounds that her presence was required by the exigencies of the pending election in West Herts, where her son was a candidate. Suffragists again were not slow to point the moral – if women were fit (and they obviously were fit) not only to advise, persuade and instruct voters how to vote, but also to conduct election campaigns from start to finish, they were surely fit to vote themselves.

The death of Queen Victoria in January 1901 called forth a spontaneous burst of loyal gratitude, devotion and appreciation from all parties and all sections of the country. Every leading statesman among her councillors dwelt on the extraordinary penetration of her mind, her wide political knowledge, her great practical sagacity, her grasp of principle, and they combined to acclaim her as the most trusted of all the constitutional monarchs whom the world had then seen. How could she be all that they justly claimed for her, if the whole female sex laboured under the disabilities which, according to Mrs Humphry Ward, were imposed by Nature and therefore irremedi-able? Nevertheless, it must not be supposed, genuine as were these tributes to Queen Victoria's political sagacity, that her example immediately cleared out of the minds of the opponents the notion that women were fitly classed with aliens, felons, idiots and lunatics, as persons who, for reasons of public safety, were debarred from the exercise of the Parliamentary franchise.

The Parliament returned in 1906 had an immense Liberal majority. There were only 157 Unionist members in the House of Commons against 513 Liberals, Labour men and Nationalists, all of whom were for Home Rule and therefore prepared to support in all critical divisions the new administration which was formed under the Premiership of Sir Henry Campbell Bannerman.* The new House contained 426 members pledged to women's suffrage. The Premier was himself a suffragist, but his Cabinet contained several determined anti-suffragists, notable among whom were Mr Herbert H. Asquith, Chancellor of the Exchequer,* and Mr James Bryce,* Chief Secretary for Ireland (now Lord Bryce), who became British Ambassador to the United States in 1907. The new Prime Minister received a large, representative suffrage deputation in May 1906, in which all sections of suffragist opinion were represented, and their case was laid before him with force and clearness. In reply he told them that they had made out 'a conclusive and irrefutable case', but that he was not prepared to take any steps to realise their hopes. When asked what he would advise ardent suffragists to do, he told them to 'go on pestering'. This advice was taken to heart by the group (a small minority of the whole) who had lately formed in Manchester the organisation known as the Women's Social and Political Union, led by Mrs Pankhurst.*

An unforeseen misfortune was the death in 1908 of Sir H.C. Bannerman and the fact that his successor was our principal opponent in the Government, Mr Asquith. It was not very long before he revealed the line of his attack upon the enfranchisement of women. He informed his party in May 1908 that his intention was to introduce before the expiration of the existing Parliament a Reform Bill giving a wide extension of the franchise to men and no franchise at all to women. In the previous February a Women's Suffrage Bill, which removed all sex disability from existing franchises, had passed its second reading in the House of Commons,* but this apparently had no effect on Mr Asquith. There were, however, some cracks in his armour. He admitted that about two thirds of his Cabinet and a majority of his party were favourable to women's suffrage, and he promised that when his own exclusively male Reform Bill was before the House and had got into committee, if an amendment to include women were moved on democratic lines, his Government, as a Government, would not oppose it. This was at all events an advance on the position taken by Mr Gladstone upon his Reform Bill of 1884, when he vehemently opposed a women's suffrage amendment and caused it to be defeated.*

The emergence of what was afterwards known as 'militancy' belongs to this period, dating from the general election of 1906, and very much stimulated by Premier Bannerman's reply to the deputation in that year and by the attitude of Mr Asquith. It will ever be an open question on which different people, with equal opportunities of forming a judgement, will pronounce different verdicts, whether 'militancy' did more harm or good to the suffrage cause.* It certainly broke down the 'conspiracy of silence' on the subject to then be observed by the press. Every extravagance, every folly, every violent expression and, of course, when the 'militants' after 1908 proceeded to acts of violence, every outrage against person or property were given the widest possible publicity, not only in Great Britain but all over the world. There was soon not an intelligent human being in any country who was not discussing women's suffrage and arguing either for or against it. This was an immense advantage to the movement, for we had, as Sir H. Campbell Bannerman had said, 'a conclusive and irrefutable case'. Our difficulty had been to get it heard and considered and this 'militancy' secured. The anti-suffrage press believed that it would kill the movement, and it was this belief which encouraged them to give it the widest possible publicity. The wilder and more extravagant the 'militants' became, the more they were quoted, described and advertised in every way. The sort of 'copy' which anti-suffrage papers demanded was supplied by them in cartloads and not at all by law-abiding suffragists, who were an immense majority of the whole. This can be illustrated by an anecdote. The constitutional suffragists* had organised a big meeting in Trafalgar Square, and had secured a strong team of first-rate speakers. The square was well filled and on the fringe of the crowd the following conversation was overheard between two press men who had come to report the proceedings. One said he was going away; the second asked why, and the first answered: 'It's no good stopping, there's no copy in this – these women are only talking sense!'

The earlier years of militant activity were, in my opinion, helpful to the whole movement, for up to 1908 the 'militants' had only adopted sensational and unusual methods, such as waving flags and making speeches in the lobby

of the House and asking inconvenient questions at public meetings. They had suffered a great deal of violence,
but had used none. From 1908 onwards, however, they
began to use violence – stone-throwing, personal attacks,
sometimes with whips – on obnoxious members of the
Government – window-smashing, the destruction of the
contents of letterboxes – in one instance the destruction
of ballot papers cast in an election. Later arson practised
for the destruction or attempted destruction of churches
and houses became more and more frequent. All this had
an intensely irritating effect on public opinion. 'Suffragist',
as far as the general public was concerned, became almost
synonymous with 'Harpy'. This cause, which had not been
defeated on a straight vote in the House of Commons since
1886, was now twice defeated, once in 1912 and once in
1913. The whole spirit engendered by attempting to gain
by violence or threats of violence what was not conceded
to justice and reason was intensely inimical to the spirit of
our movement. We believed with profound conviction that
whatever might be gained in that way did not and could
not rest on a sure foundation. The women's movement was
an appeal against government by physical force, and those
who used physical violence in order to promote it were
denying their faith to make their faith prevail.

The difference made a deep rift in the suffrage movement. The constitutional societies felt bound to exclude
'militants' from their membership, and on several occasions issued strongly worded protests against the use of
violence as political propaganda. The fact that men under

similar circumstances had been much more violent and destructive, especially in earlier days, when they were less civilised, did not inspire us with the wish to imitate them. We considered that they had been wrong and that 'direct action', as it is now the fashion to call coercion by means of physical force, had always reacted unfavourably on those who employed it. While the constitutional societies freely and repeatedly expressed their views on these points, the 'militants' not unnaturally retorted by attempting to break up our meetings, shouting down our speakers and provoking every sort of disorder at them. It was an exceptionally difficult situation, and that we won through as well as we did was due to the solid loyalty to constitutional and law-abiding methods of propaganda of the great mass of suffragists throughout the country. We quoted the American proverb, 'Three hornets can upset a camp meeting', and we determined to hold steadily on our way and not let our hornets upset us. Our societies multiplied rapidly, both in numbers and in membership. For instance, the number forming the National Union of Women's Suffrage Societies increased from 64 in 1909 to 130 in 1910, and went on increasing rapidly until just before the war in 1914 they numbered more than 600, with a revenue of over 42,000 pounds a year.

More important in many ways than the 'militant' movement was the emergence at the general election in 1906 of the Labour Party. Mr Keir Hardie, Mr Philip Snowden* and others of its leaders were very strong supporters of women's suffrage, and it was not long before the party definitely made the enfranchisement of women on the same terms as men a plank in its platform. In anticipation of the first general election of 1910, the NUWSS addressed the leaders of the three British parties, Conservative, Liberal and Labour, asking them what they were prepared to do for women's suffrage. Mr Asquith gave his answer at an Albert Hall meeting in December 1909. He reiterated his intention, if returned to power, of bringing in a Reform Bill, and he promised to make the insertion of a women's suffrage amendment an open question for the House of Commons to decide. He added: 'The Government... has no disposition or desire to burke the question; it is clearly an issue on which the new House ought to be given an opportunity to express its views.' This meant that the Government whips would not be put on to oppose the enfranchisement of women. Mr Balfour* replied to our memorial that it was a non-party question on which members of the Unionist Party could exercise individual freedom of action. Mr Arthur Henderson,* for the Labour Party, told us that it had already placed the enfranchisement of women on its programme. The Labour Party was not large, but it was an important advantage to us to have even a small party definitely pledged to our support. There were two general elections in 1910, in January and December. The Liberal, Labour and Nationalist group lost heavily in the second of these elections, their majority being reduced from 334 to 124.

The Labour Party between these two elections had lost six seats, but they were still forty strong, all definitely pledged to women's suffrage in the new Parliament which assembled in January, 1911. Our bill had been carried on its second reading in 1910 by a majority of 110, but after the second general election of 1910 it secured on the 5th of May 1911 a majority of 167; there were 55 pairs, only 88 members of Parliament going into the lobby* against us. The bill on each of these occasions was of a very limited character; it proposed to enfranchise women householders, widows and spinsters, and would only have added about a million women to the Parliamentary register. It was called the Conciliation Bill, because it sought to conciliate the differences between different types of suffragists in the House of Commons, from the extreme Conservative who only cared for the representation of women of property, to the extreme Radical who demanded the enfranchisement of every woman. A committee was formed to promote the success of this bill in Parliament, of which the Earl of Lytton was Chairman and Mr H.N. Brailsford Hon. Sec.* It was believed that the bill represented the greatest common measure of the House of Commons' belief in women's votes. The Labour Party were strongly in favour of a much wider enfranchisement of women, but generously waived their own preferences in order, as they believed, to get some sort of representation for women on the Statute Book. Almost immediately after this large majority for the second reading of the Conciliation Bill in May 1911, an official announcement was made by the Government that Mr Asquith's promise of the previous November that an opportunity should be afforded for proceeding with the bill in all its stages would be fulfilled in the session of 1912.

We were then in the most favourable position we had ever occupied; the passing of the Women's Suffrage Bill in the near future seemed a certainty. The 'militants' had suspended all their methods of violence in order to give the Conciliation Bill a chance, and, as just described, it had passed its second reading debate with a majority of 167, and time for 'proceeding effectively' with a similar bill in all its stages had been promised. All the suffrage societies were working harmoniously for the same bill, and the Women's Liberal Federation were co-operating with the suffrage societies, when suddenly, like a bolt from the blue, Mr Asquith dealt us a characteristic blow. In reply to a deputation from the People's Suffrage Federation early in November he announced his intention of introducing during the coming session of 1912 the Electoral Reform Bill which he had foreshadowed in 1908; he said that in this bill all existing franchises would be swept away, plural voting abolished and the period of residence reduced. The new franchise to be created was, he added, to be based on citizenship, and votes were to be given to 'citizens of full age and competent understanding', but no mention was made of the enfranchisement of women. On being asked what he intended to do about women's votes, he dismissed the subject with the remark that his opinions on the subject were well known and had suffered no change, but he reiterated the promise of 'facilities' for the Conciliation Bill in the 1912 session.

The situation, therefore, was briefly this: an agitation of ever-growing intensity and determination had for some years been carried on by women for their own enfranchisement, and no agitation at all had been manifested by men for more votes for themselves; the Prime Minister's response to this situation was to promise legislation giving far larger and wider representation to men and none at all to women. No wonder that he provoked an immediate outburst of militancy! Stones were thrown and windows smashed all along the Strand, Piccadilly, Whitehall and Bond Street, and members of the Government went about in perpetual apprehension of personal assault.

The indignation of the constitutional suffragists and of the Women's Liberal Federation with Mr Asquith was quite as real as that of the suffragettes, but it sought a different method of expression. Some knowledge of this probably reached him, as for the first time in our experience all the suffrage societies and the WLF were invited by the Prime Minister to form a deputation to him on the subject. What we were accustomed to was sending an urgent demand to him to receive us in a deputation and to get his reply that he believed 'no useful purpose would be served' by yielding to our request; but now, in November 1911, he was inviting us to come and see him! Of course we went. His whole demeanour was much more conciliatory than it had ever been before. He acknowledged the strength and intensity of the demand of women for representation, and admitted that in opposing it he was in a minority both in his Cabinet and in his party; finally he added that, although his personal opinions on the subject prevented him from initiating and proposing the change which women were pressing for, he was prepared to bow to and acquiesce in the considered judgement of the House of Commons, and he stated that this course was quite in accordance with the best traditions of English public life. The National Union of Women's Suffrage Societies, of which I was the mouthpiece, then put the following questions:

1 Is it the intention of the Government that the Reform Bill shall go through all its stages in 1912?
2 Will the bill be drafted in such a way as to admit of amendments introducing women on other terms than men?
3 Will the Government undertake not to oppose such amendments?
4 Will the Government regard any amendment enfranchising women which is carried as an integral part of the bill be defended by the Government in all its later stages?

To all these questions, as they were put severally, Mr Asquith replied 'Yes, certainly.'

Mr Lloyd George, who was present, was pressed by the deputation to speak, but did so only very briefly. He was known as an opponent of the Conciliation Bill, but had voted for it in 1911 because it was so drafted as to admit of free amendment. He made no secret of his conviction that the wider enfranchisement afforded by amendment of the Government measure would, to use his own expression, 'torpedo' the Conciliation Bill. Almost immediately after the deputation thus described he sent the following message to the NUWSS: 'The Prime Minister's pronouncement as to the attitude to be adopted by the Government towards the question seems to make the carrying of a Women's Suffrage Amendment to next year's Franchise Bill a certainty. I am willing to do all in my power to help those who are labouring to reach a successful issue in the coming session. Next year provides the supreme opportunity and nothing but unwise handling of that chance can compass failure.'

There was plenty of unwise handling, but not, as I am proud to think, from the constitutional suffragists. The first was the wild outburst of 'militancy' already referred to. Mr Lloyd George was pursued by persistent interruption and annoyance deliberately organised by the Women's Social and Political Union. A meeting he addressed at Bath, mainly devoted to advocacy of women's suffrage, on the 24th of November 1911, was all but turned into a bear garden by these deliberately planned and very noisy interruptions. Not to be outdone in 'unwise handling', Mr Asquith next had his innings. He received an anti-suffrage deputation on the 14th of December 1911, about three weeks after he had received the suffragists, and in the course of his remarks to them he said: 'As an individual I am in entire agreement with you that the grant of the Parliamentary vote to women in this country would be a political mistake of a very disastrous kind.' This went far to invalidate the fair-seeming promises to us given about three weeks earlier. How could a man in the all-important position of Prime Minister pledge himself to use all the forces at the disposal of the Government to pass in all its stages through both houses a measure which might include the perpetration of 'a political mistake of a very disastrous kind'? A member of Mr Asquith's own party who took part in the anti-suffrage deputation interpreted this expression of his chief as an SOS call to his follow- ers in the House to deliver him from the humiliation of having to fulfil the promises he had given us. Every kind of intrigue and trick known to the accomplished parliament- arian was put into operation. Every Irish Nationalist vote was detached from support of the bill. A description of one of these discreditable devices, among them an attempt to hold up the NUWSS to public contempt as purveyors of 'obscene' literature, will be found in a book by myself called *The Women's Victory and After,** published in 1920.

The first result of these intrigues was the defeat of the Conciliation Bill, by 14 votes only, on the 28th of March 1912. This was hailed as an immense triumph by the anti-suffragists, as indeed, in a sense, it was, for exactly the same bill had been carried by the same House in 1911 by a majority of 167; but it was a triumph which cost the victors dear, especially when the tricks and perversions of truth came to light by which it had been achieved. From this time forward public opinion was more decided in our favour and the general view was that the Government had treated us shabbily.

The progress made by the Government in pressing forward their Electoral Reform Bill was not rapid. When it was at last introduced it was discovered to be not a Reform Bill, but in the main a Registration Bill. In the second reading debate Mr Asquith described his bill as one to enfranchise 'male persons only', and said in regard to women that he could not conceive that the House would 'so far stultify itself as to reverse the considered judgement it had already arrived at' earlier in the session. It was a 'considered judgement' to defeat the bill by 14 votes in 1912, but not a 'considered judgement' to have it carried by 167 in 1911! Sir Edward Grey* felt strongly that the House had placed itself in a very undesirable position, but the Conciliation Bill was defeated and Sir Edward Grey, Mr Lloyd George and the leading suffragists in the Government continued to assure us that the inclusion of women's suffrage through an amendment of the Government Bill presented us with by far the best prospect of success we had ever had. We worked as we had never worked before to secure the success of this amendment or series of amendments. The session of 1912 had lasted from January to December without the committee stage of the Government Bill being reached. This interminable session overflowed into 1913 and the debate on the suffrage amendments of the Government Bill was dated to begin on the 24th of January of that year. On the 23rd of January, however, in reply to a question, the Speaker (Mr Lowther) indicated that he would probably be compelled to rule that if the bill were amended so as to include the enfranchisement of women, he might feel obliged to rule that in this form it was not the same bill of which the second reading had been carried in July, and it would, therefore, have to be withdrawn and re-introduced!* This ruling he confirmed on the following Monday, the 27th of January. Therefore, every one of the fair promises which Mr Asquith had given us in November 1911 proved to be absolutely worthless.

I do not accuse Mr Asquith of anything worse at this stage than blundering. He was manifestly confounded and distressed by the Speaker's ruling.* Whether this were due to the naming of the bill or to Mr Asquith's own speech on the second reading, 'This is a bill to enfranchise male persons only, etc.', we were not able to discover; but the net result was that he found himself in a position in which it was impossible for him to fulfil the promises he had given us. Under these circumstances he did not take the only honourable course open to him, i.e. of sending for us once more and asking us what we should consider a reasonable equivalent for these unredeemed promises. He had made these promises five years back and had repeated them from time to time ever since. Now they were null and void. The only reasonable equivalent would have been the introduction of a Government Reform Bill which included the enfranchisement of women. Probably Mr Asquith knew that this was what we should urge, for he not only did not send for us, but he refused to see us or consult us in any way. He tossed us, without our consent, the thoroughly worthless substitute of a day for a Private Member's Bill, such as we had had experience of time and again ever since 1870. The NUWSS indignantly rejected this offer and took no interest in the proposed bill, which was, however, introduced and given a day for second reading in May 1913, when it was defeated by a majority of 47.

This discreditable series of incidents did far more harm to the Government than to the suffrage cause, as was very conclusively shown in the press. *Punch*, for instance, had a cartoon on the 5th of February 1913 representing a dance in which Mr Asquith figured as a defaulting partner in a corner and trying to escape from an indignant woman who said, 'You've cut my dance!' This was indicative of the general trend of public opinion.

In the previous year the NUWSS had placed a new interpretation on its election policy. This was to support in elections irrespective of party 'the best friend of women's suffrage'. After the defeat of the Conciliation Bill in 1912, when 42 so-called 'friends' voted against it, we resolved in the future that the best friend was a man who was not only personally satisfactory but who also belonged to a party which had made women's suffrage a plank in its platform. This meant support for the Labour Party, and for the development of this policy we raised a special fund called the Election Fighting Fund, and took active steps in canvassing and speaking for Labour men whenever they presented themselves as candidates for vacant seats. Our movement had now become the storm centre of English politics. A well-known Labour leader wrote of the political situation in February 1913 as follows: 'The women's suffrage question will now dominate British politics until it is settled. It has within the last few weeks killed a great Government measure, and it has done more than that. It has made it impossible for this or any succeeding Liberal Government to deal with franchise reform without giving votes to women. The Labour Party will see to that.'

In 1913 the NUWSS organised the greatest public demonstration it had ever made. We called it the Pilgrimage. It meant processions of non-militant suffragists, wearing their badges and carrying banners, marching towards London along eight of the great trunk roads. These eight processions, many of them lasting several weeks, stopped at towns and villages on their way, held meetings, distributed literature and collected funds. It was all a tremendous and unprecedented success, well organised and well done throughout (described in detail in *The Women's Victory*). The Pilgrimage made a very great impression and was favourably commented on in the organs of the press, which had never helped us before. We finished the Pilgrimage with a mass meeting in Hyde Park on the 26th of July, where we had seventeen platforms, one for each of our federations. We asked Mr Asquith and the leaders of other political parties to receive a deputation from the Pilgrimage the following week. They all accepted, with the exception of Mr John Redmond.* When Mr Asquith received us his demeanour was far less unfriendly than it had ever been before. He admitted that the offer of a Private Member's Bill was no equivalent for the loss of a place in a Government Bill. He said: 'Proceed as you have been proceeding, continue to the end,' and said if we could show that 'a substantial majority of the country was favourable to women's suffrage, Parliament would yield, as it had always hitherto done, to the opinion of the country.'

In May 1914, suffrage ground was broken in the House of Lords by Lord Selborne* and Lord Lytton, who introduced a bill on the lines of the Conciliation Bill, the latter making one of the most powerful speeches in our support to which we had ever listened. The bill was rejected by 104 to 60, but we were more than satisfied by the weight of the speeches on our side and by the effect produced by them. Another important event which greatly helped our movement in 1914 was the protest of the National Trade Union Congress on the 12th of February against the Government's failure to redeem its repeated pledges to women and demanding 'a Government Reform Bill which must include the enfranchisement of women'. This was followed by resolutions passed at the annual conference of the National Labour Party re-affirming its decision 'to oppose any further extension of the franchise to men in which women were not included'.

There must, according to law, have been a general election in 1915, and the remarkable progress of the women's cause made us feel confident that a Parliament would be elected deeply pledged to our support. Our friends were being elected and our enemies, including that worst type of enemy, the false friend and the so-called Liberal afraid of his own principles, were being rejected at by-elections in a manner that foreshadowed a great gain to suffrage forces at the general election. Then suddenly, destroying all our hopes of success and jeopardising the very existence of representative government and all forms of democracy throughout the world, came the outbreak of war; the entry of our own country and the resulting concentration of the vast majority of the British people, whether men or women, in the gigantic national effort which the successful resistance of such a foe demanded. The 4th of August 1914 was a heart-breaking day for us. Nevertheless, suffragists from the first faced the facts and saw clearly what their duty was. The 'militants' instantly abandoned every sort of violence. A large number of the more active members of their societies formed the Women's Emergency Corps, who were ready to undertake all kinds of national work which the exigencies of the situation demanded. The NUWSS Executive Committee meeting on the 3rd of August, the day before our own country was actually involved, resolved to suspend immediately all political propaganda for its own ends. Under normal circumstances we should have summoned a council meeting to discuss the situation and to determine the course to be taken by the Union. This being impossible, owing to difficulties connected with railway communication, we consulted our societies, then numbering over five hundred, by post, placing them in possession of our own views, viz. that ordinary political work would have to be suspended during the war, and suggesting that our best course would be to use our staff and organising capacity in promoting forms of work designed to mitigate the distress caused by the war. We felt that our members would desire to be of service to the nation and that the NUWSS had in their organisation a special gift which they could offer to their country. This view was endorsed by our societies, with only two dissenting.

On receiving this practically unanimous backing we further proceeded to recommend distinct forms of active service. The Local Government Board had addressed a circular to lord mayors and mayors and chairmen of town and county councils, directing them at once to form local relief committees to deal with any kind of distress caused by the war. We suggested to our societies that they should offer their services to help, each in its own district, in this national work. We also opened in different parts of the country forty workrooms in which women thrown out of work by the war found employment. We established bureaux for the registration of voluntary workers, and gradually our work spread in all directions: help for the Belgian refugees, the starting of clubs and canteens for soldiers and sailors, clubs for soldiers' wives, work in connection with the Sailors' and Soldiers' Families Association, patrol work in the neighbourhood of soldiers' training camps, Red Cross work, conducting French classes for our men in training. A very large number of our societies concentrated on maternity and child welfare work; others in country districts took up fruit picking and preserving in order to conserve the national food supplies. It is really impossible to mention all our various activities. These were included under a general heading adopted at a provincial council meeting held in November 1914, urging 'our societies and all members of the Union to continue by every means in their power all efforts which had for their object the sustaining of the vital energies of the nation so long as such special efforts may be required.'

The war work with which the name of the NUWSS is most widely known was the formation of the Scottish Women's Hospitals for Foreign Service. This was initiated and organised by the Hon. Sec. of our Scottish Federation, Dr Elsie Inglis,* and was backed by the whole of the NUWSS (see *Life of Dr E. Inglis* by Lady Frances Balfour).* Meeting at first with persistent snubbing from the Royal Army Medical Corps and the British Red Cross, Dr Inglis formed her first hospital at the Royaumont Abbey,* about thirty miles from Paris, officered entirely by women. Other units on similar lines quickly followed in France and Serbia. Their work was magnificent, and was rapidly recognised as such by the military authorities and by all who came in contact with it. These hospitals probably produced by the example of their high standard of professional efficiency and personal devotion a permanent influence on the development of the women's movement in those countries where they were located. They received no farthing of Government money, but raised the 428,856 pounds, which their audited accounts show as their net total to the 3rd of August 1919, entirely by private subscription from all over the world, including, of course, the United States.

95

The NUWSS were very early in the field of women's national work during the war, because their members were already organised and accustomed to work together, but it is no exaggeration to say that the whole of the women of the country, of all classes, suffragist and anti-suffragist, threw themselves into work for the nation in a way that had never been anticipated by those who had judged women by pre-war standards. Into munition work and all kinds of manufacturing activity they crowded in their thousands. They worked on the land and undertook many kinds of labour that had hitherto been supposed to be beyond their strength and capacity. By what was called the Treasury Agreement of 1915, the trade unions were induced to suspend the operation of their rules excluding the employment of female labour. They bargained that women should be paid the same as men for the same output, and the Government agreed not to use the women as a reservoir of cheap labour. Thus industrial liberty was ensured for women – at least so long as the war should last.

All these things combined to produce an enormous effect on public opinion. Newspapers were full of the praises of women; financiers, statesmen, economists and politicians declared that without the aid of women it would be impossible to win the war. The anti-suffragism of Mr Asquith even was beginning to crumble. In speaking of the heroic death of Edith Cavell in Belgium in October 1915,* he said: 'She has taught the bravest men among us a supreme lesson of courage; yes... and there are thousands of such women, and a year ago we did not know it.' Almost the whole of the press was on our side. The general tone was that it would be difficult to refuse woman a voice in the control of affairs after the splendid way in which she had justified her claim to it. We old suffragists felt that we were living in a new world where everyone agreed with us. Nevertheless, I do not believe we should have won the vote just when we did if it had not been that, through the action of the Government itself, it was absolutely necessary to introduce legislation in order to prevent the almost total disfranchisement of many millions of men who had been serving their country abroad in the navy and army, or in munition or other work which had withdrawn them from the places where they usually resided.

It may be necessary to explain to non-British readers that by far the most important qualification for the Parliamentary franchise in this country before 1918 was the occupation of premises, and before a man could be put on the register of voters it was necessary for its owner to prove 'occupation' of these premises for twelve months previous to the last 15th of July. Seven out of every eight voters were placed on the register through this qualification. It was not a property qualification, for the tiniest cottage at a shilling a week could qualify its occupier for a vote if he had fulfilled the condition just described; and a man might be a millionaire without getting a vote if he were not in occupation of qualifying premises. Before the war the register of voters was kept up to date by annual revision. The war, however, made this difficult, and the

Government in 1915 gave directions that this annual revision should be abandoned. As the war went on, the existing register, therefore, rapidly became more and more out of date. Millions of the best men in the country had become disqualified through their war service by giving up their qualifying premises. The House of Commons again and again postponed the date of the general election, but the occasional by-elections which took place proved that there was no register in existence on which it would be morally possible to appeal to the country. The old, the feeble, the slacker, the crank, the conscientious objector would all be left in full strength, and the fighting men would be disfranchised. A Parliament elected on such a register would, Mr Asquith declared, be wholly lacking in moral authority. Therefore, by sheer necessity, the Government was forced to introduce legislation dealing with the whole franchise question as it affected the male voter. A coalition Government of the Liberal, Conservative and Labour parties had been formed in 1915. This improved suffrage prospects, for many of the new men joining the Government, more especially Lord Robert Cecil,* the Earl of Selborne and the Earl of Lytton, were warm supporters of our cause; while, in making room for these newcomers, Mr Asquith found it possible to dispense with the services of men of the type of Sir Charles Hobhouse, Mr J.A. Pease* and others who were our opponents. The formation of a coalition Government helped us in another way. Neither of the great parties, Conservative and Liberal, had been unanimous on the women's question, and the heads of these parties lived in terror of smashing up their party by pledging themselves to definite action on our side. Mr Gladstone had broken up the Liberal Party in 1886 by advocating Irish Home Rule, and Mr Balfour and Mr Chamberlain had broken up the Conservative Party by advocating Protection in 1903–04. Each of these had, in consequence, a prolonged sojourn in the wilderness of Opposition. But now a Government was formed in which all the parties were represented, except the Irish Nationalists, who had refused to join, and therefore our friends in both the old parties could give free rein to their disposition to make women's suffrage a reality without dread of bringing disaster on their organisations. The attitude of the NUWSS, and seventeen other con-stitutional suffrage societies who had united to form a Consultative Committee, was quite clear as to the line we should take under these circumstances. In various ways, and by repeated communications, letters, memorials and deputations, we kept the Government informed that if their intentions with regard to the new register were lim-ited simply to replacing upon it the names of the men who had lost their vote through their patriotic service, we should not press our own claim; but if, on the other hand, the Government determined to proceed by creating a new basis for the franchise, or changing the law in any way which would result in the addition of a large number of men to the register without doing anything for women, we should use every means in our power within the limits of lawful agitation to bring the case for the enfranchisement of women before Parliament and the country.

Mr Asquith answered a communication from us on these lines in May 1916 with the greatest politeness, but said that 'no such legislation was at present in contemplation'. However, within the next fortnight it was in contemplation, and the Government made repeated attempts to deal with the situation by the creation of a special register. All the attempts were rejected by the House of Commons, which evidently wanted the subject dealt with on broader and more comprehensive lines. On the 14th of August Mr Asquith, in introducing yet another Special Register Bill, announced his conversion to women's suffrage! This was an advent of great importance to our movement, for it virtually made the Liberal Party a suffrage party, but the Parliamentary difficulty was not removed, for the Government was still nibbling at the question by trying to deal with it by little amendments to the law relating to the registration of voters. At last a way out was devised. Mr Walter Long,* President of the Local Government Board, a typical conservative country gentleman and at that time an anti-suffragist, made the suggestion that the whole question of electoral reform, including the enfranchisement of women, should be referred to a non-party conference, consisting of members of both Houses of Parliament and presided over by the Speaker. Mr Asquith concurred and Parliament agreed. Women's suffrage was only one of many subjects connected with electoral reform which had to be dealt with by the conference, but it is not too much to say that if it had not been for the urgency of the claim of women to representation the conference would never have been brought into existence.

The members of this conference were chosen by the Speaker, who was careful to give equal representation to suffragists and anti-suffragists. Sir John Simon and Sir Willoughby Dickinson,* members of the conference, were very active and skilful in organising the forces in our favour. The conference was called into being in October 1916, and began its sittings at once. A ministerial crisis which occurred in December resulted in the resignation of Mr Asquith and the appointment of Mr Lloyd George as his successor. The Speaker enquired of the new Prime Minister if he desired the conference to continue its labours. The reply was an emphatic affirmative. The conference reported on the 27th of January 1917. Everyone knows that it recommended by a majority – some said a large majority – the granting of some measure of suffrage to women. Put as briefly as possible, the franchise recommended for women was 'household franchise', and for the purposes of the bill a woman was reckoned to be a householder not only if she was so in her own right, but if she were the wife of a householder. An age limit of thirty was imposed upon women, not because it was in any way logical or reasonable, but simply and solely in order to produce a constituency in which the men were not outnumbered by the women.

Some few weeks earlier we had heard on unimpeachable authority that the new Prime Minister was 'very keen and very practical' on our question and was prepared to introduce legislation upon it without delay. He no doubt remembered how emphatically he had told us in 1911 of the extreme value of the promises which had been made to us by Mr Asquith, and how in our meeting in the Albert Hall in the following March he had referred to the doubt which some suffragists had expressed upon the worth of these promises as 'an imputation of deep dishonour which he absolutely declined to contemplate'. He had in 1911 put into writing and sent as a message to *The Common Cause*, the official organ of the NUWSS,* a statement of his conviction that Mr Asquith's promises made the carrying of a women's suffrage amendment to next year's franchise bill a certainty, and he had offered his personal help to bring this about. It has already been described how all these confident hopes had been brought to nought; but now, December 1916, within a fortnight of becoming Prime Minister, Mr Lloyd George let us know that he was not only ready but keen to go forward on practical lines. When Parliament met we asked the Prime Minister to receive a large and representative deputation of women who had worked for their country during the war. Our object was to ask him to legislate at once on the lines recommended by the Speaker's conference, but we were pushing an open door.

The new Prime Minister had arranged to receive us on the 29th of March 1917, and on the 28th Mr Asquith had moved a resolution in the House of Commons, and his motion had been agreed to by 341 votes to 62, calling for the early introduction of legislation based on the recommendations of the Speaker's conference. When our deputation waited on Mr Lloyd George the following day, he was able to inform us that he had already instructed the Government draftsman to draw up a bill on these lines. The debate in the House on the 28th of March had turned mainly on women's suffrage, and the immense majority in support of Mr Asquith's motion was rightly regarded as a suffrage triumph. Every leader of every party in the House of Commons had taken part in the debate and had expressed his support of the enfranchisement of women. The Government whips had not been put on,* and throughout the debates which followed the bill was not treated as a Government but as a House of Commons measure. The victory, therefore, was all the more welcome to us, because it was the result of a free vote of the House. Mr Asquith's retraction of his former errors was quite handsome. He said, among other things, that his 'eyes which for years in this matter had been clouded by fallacies and sealed by illusions at last had been opened to the truth.' It required a European war on the vastest scale that the world had ever known to shake him out of his fallacies and illusions, and many of us felt that it would have been better if a less terrible convulsion had sufficed to awaken him; but still, now he was awakened, he was prompt in owning he had been in the wrong, and therefore no more was to be said. The subsequent stages of this Representation of the People Bill were a series of triumphs for the suffrage cause. The second reading debate was taken on the 22nd and 23rd of May, and again turned almost entirely on the women's question; the majority was 329 to 40. When the bill was in committee and the clauses enfranchising women were taken up on the 19th of June, the majority was 385 to 55, or exactly seven to one. On the 20th of June a last division was made, when the number of anti-suffragists was only 17.

Our friends in the Speaker's conference had so often impressed on us the danger of departing, even in the direction of obvious improvement, from its recommendations that we had carefully abstained from urging any deviation from them; but when the immense majorities just quoted showed that the bill and our clauses in it were safe beyond a peradventure, we did press very strongly that the same principle should be applied to municipal suffrage for women which had already been sanctioned by the House for the Parliamentary suffrage, namely that the wives of householders should be recognised as householders, which would entitle them to vote. On the 15th of November an amendment to this effect was moved, but was not accepted by the Government. There were vigorous protests in our favour from all parts of the House, and the debate on it was adjourned. During the interval the NUWSS and other societies with whom we were co-operating bombarded the leader of the House and the minister in charge of the bill with letters and telegrams in support of the amendment. These produced a good effect, and on the 20th of November, Government opposition having been withdrawn, the amendment was agreed to without a division. Thus, without the existence of a single woman voter, but on the strength of her coming into existence within the next few months, the women on the municipal registers of Great Britain and Ireland were increased in number from about one million to over eight and a half millions. And yet Lord Bryce and the other anti-suffragists assured us that the vote would make no difference!

In the House of Commons a third reading of the Representation of the People Bill was taken on the 7th of December without a division. The bill was now safely through the Commons, but its passage through the Lords had yet to be undertaken. The second reading debate began on the 17th of December, and lasted two days. No one could predict what would happen; Lord Curzon,* president of the Anti-Suffrage League, was leader of the House and chief representative of the Government. The Lord Chancellor (Lord Finlay),* who is in the chair in House of Lords' debates, was an envenomed opponent. Among other influential peers whom we knew as our enemies were Lord Lansdowne, Lord Halsbury, Lord Balfour of Burleigh and Lord Bryce. On the other hand, we could count on the support of Lord Selborne, Lord Lytton, the Archbishop of Canterbury, the Bishop of London, Lord Courtney and Lord Milner.* We looked forward to the debate and the divisions in the Lords with considerable trepidation. The Lords have no constituents; they have no seats to fight for and defend. It is therefore impossible to influence them by any electioneering arts, but we sent to all the peers a carefully worded and influentially signed memorandum setting forth the chief facts and arguments in our favour. The second reading of the bill was taken in the Lords without a division, the most important speech against it being Lord Bryce's; he insisted again and again that the possession of a vote made no difference. Lord Sydenham* had the courage (!) to assert that the suffrage movement had made no progress in America, and, while admitting that it had lately been adopted in the State of New York, no doubt thought that he was giving a fair description when he said: 'In America... fourteen states have refused the franchise to women and two, Montana and Nevada, have granted it. The population of the fourteen states is 43,000,000, and that of the two states is 500,000.' (Twelve states had fully enfranchised their women.)

The real fight in the House of Lords began on the 8th of January 1918, when the committee stage was reached. The debate lasted three days, and on Clause IV, which enfranchised women, Lord Selborne made an extraordinarily powerful and eloquent speech in its favour. The House was filled, and the excitement on both sides was intense. As we were sitting crowded in the small pen allotted to ladies not peeresses in the Upper House on the 10th of January, we received a cable saying the House of Representatives in Washington had accepted the Women's Suffrage Amendment to the Federal Constitution by the necessary two-thirds majority. This we hailed as a good omen. No one knew what Lord Sydenham thought of it! The most exciting moment was when Lord Curzon rose to close the debate. The first part of his speech was devoted to a description of the disasters which he believed would follow from the adoption of women's franchise, but the second part was occupied by giving very good reasons for not voting against it. He reminded their Lordships of the immense majorities by which it had been supported in the House of Commons, by majorities in every party 'including those to which most of your Lordships belong... Your Lordships can vote as you please; you can cut this clause out of the bill – you have a perfect right to do so – but if you think that by killing the clause you can also save the bill, I believe you to be mistaken... The House of Commons will return it to you with the clause re-inserted. Will you be prepared to put it back...?' Before he sat down, Lord Curzon announced his intention of not voting at all, for the reason that if he had done otherwise he 'might be accused of having precipitated a conflict from which your Lordships could not emerge with credit.' The division was taken almost immediately after the conclusion of this speech. Both of the archbishops and the twelve bishops present voted for the bill. Our clause was carried by 134 votes to 71, and women's suffrage was, therefore, supported in the Lords by nearly two to one. The Lords inserted in it among other things Proportional Representation. It was on this and not on women's suffrage that the final contest took place when it was returned to the Commons, but at last the long struggle of women for free citizenship was ended, having continued a little over fifty years. The huge majorities by which we had won in the House of Commons had afforded our ship deep water enough to float safely over the rocks and reefs of the House of Lords. The Royal Assent was given on the 6th of February 1918.

The first election at which women voted was held on the 14th of December. Our friends in the Speaker's conference had aimed at producing a constituency numbering roughly about 10,000,000 men and 6,000,000 women. The actual numbers of both sexes enfranchised by the Act of 1918 turned out to be considerably in excess of this calculation. A Parliamentary return published in November 1918 showed the following numbers of men and women on the register.

	Men
	12,913,166
Naval and military voters	3,896,763
	16,809,929

	Women
	8,479,156
Naval and military voters	3,372
	8,482,528

At the annual council meeting of the National Union of Women's Suffrage Societies held in March 1918, its object was changed by formal vote. It was no longer necessary to concentrate on women's suffrage, and we adopted as our object, 'To obtain all such reforms as are necessary to secure a real equality of liberties, status and opportunities between men and women.' No change of name was made until the following year, when a revised constitution was adopted and the name was modified in accordance with our present object. We have now become the National Union of Societies for Equal Citizenship, and we hope that the letters NUSEC will soon become as familiar and as dear to our members as NUWSS were in the old days. At the same meeting I retired from the presidency and my friend and colleague, Miss Eleanor Rathbone,* was elected in my place.

In 1907* Acts of Parliament for England, Wales and Scotland (and one for Ireland in 1911) made women eligible as members of town, county, burgh and borough councils and as chairmen of these bodies, including the right to be mayors and provosts, aldermen and baillies, with the limitation that women appointed to an office carrying with it the right to be justices of the peace should be incapacitated from so acting. These acts, though non-contentious in the party sense, required fourteen years' strenuous work to secure their adoption as Government measures. This was achieved during Sir Henry Campbell Bannerman's premiership, the necessary legislation being announced in the King's Speech as part of the Government programme.

In 1918 the Qualification of Women Act for the United Kingdom made women eligible to the House of Commons. The bill passed almost without opposition through both Houses and became law in the week ending the 16th of November. As the general election took place on the 14th of December, there was little time for preparation; nevertheless, there were seventeen women candidates and one, the Countess Markievicz,* a Sinn Feiner, was elected, but refused to take her seat. The fact that her husband was a foreigner made it doubtful whether she would have been allowed to do so, though an Irishwoman by birth. In 1919 Viscountess Astor* was elected for Plymouth.

In 1919 the Sex Disqualification Removal Act for the United Kingdom went some way – but not the whole way – towards the fulfilment of the pledge given by the coalition Government of Mr Lloyd George in December 1918, 'to remove existing inequalities in the law as between men and women'. A much more complete bill had been introduced by the Labour Party early in the session, which passed through all its stages in the House of Commons notwithstanding Government opposition, but was defeated in the House of Lords and the Government changeling substituted. This act, though it did not give women the parliamentary vote on the same terms as men, nor admit them to the civil service on equal terms, and though the clause specifically conferring on them eligibility to the House of Lords was cut out, contained, nevertheless, important provisions in the direction of equality. It allowed them to sit on juries, be justices of the peace, sworn in as police officers, enter the legal profession and made it possible for the universities of Oxford and Cambridge to admit women to membership and degrees on equal terms with men.

The only important advance in education after 1900 was the throwing open to women by the governing body of Trinity College, Dublin of degrees, membership and all privileges pertaining thereto in 1903. All the universities in the United Kingdom, with the exception of Oxford and Cambridge, have been for many years open to women, and in November 1919 a royal commission was appointed to inquire into their financial resources and into the administration and application of these resources. On the commission, Miss Penrose of Somerville College, Oxford,* and Miss B.A. Clough of Newnham College, Cambridge,* the women's colleges, were appointed as members. An act of Parliament later enabled both universities to grant membership, degrees and all privileges to women. Oxford availed itself of these powers without delay. Cambridge, in December 1920, refused to do so by a large vote, but it will ultimately have to open its doors.*

APPENDIX

Nebraska Men's Association Opposed to Woman Suffrage

To the electors of the State of Nebraska:
At a meeting of men lately held in the city of Omaha the following resolution was unanimously adopted:

Resolved: That it is the sense of this meeting that a manifesto be prepared, issued and circulated, setting forth the reasons for our opposition to the pending constitutional amendment providing for equal (woman) suffrage and requesting the co-operation of the voters of the state, and that such manifesto be signed by all the men present.

We yield to none in our admiration, veneration and respect for woman. We recognise in her admirable and adorable qualities and sweet and noble influences which make for the betterment of mankind and the advancement of civilisation. We have ever been willing and ready

113

to grant to woman every right and protection, even to favouritism in the law, and to give her every opportunity that makes for development and true womanhood. We have a full appreciation of all the great things which have been accomplished by women in education, in charity and in benevolent work and in other channels of duty too numerous to mention, by which both men and women have been benefited, society improved and the welfare of the human race advanced. We would take from women none of their privileges as citizens, but we do not believe that women are adapted to the political work of the world.

The discussion of all questions growing out of the social and family relations and local economic conditions has no direct relationship to the right of women to participate in the political affairs of government. The right of suffrage does not attach of right to the owners of property, for, if so, all other persons should be disfranchised. It is not a fundamental right of taxpayers, for a great body of men are not taxpayers, and nine-tenths of the women who would become voters, if woman suffrage were adopted, would be non-taxpayers. It is not an inherent right of citizenship, for the time never was in the whole history of the world when the franchise was granted to all citizens... Franchise is a privilege of government granted only to those to whom the Government sees fit to grant it. As a law-abiding people men and women alike should recognise once and for all that the right of suffrage is not a natural or inherent right of citizenship but can only come by grant from the Government.

We must also recognise that woman suffrage is inconsistent with the fundamental principles upon which our representative government was founded, and to accept it now involves revolutionary changes. The framers of the federal constitution, a body of the wisest men the country has ever produced, did not recognise or provide for woman suffrage. No one of the original thirteen states which adopted it provided in their constitutions for woman suffrage. True, it was permitted in New Jersey from 1776 to 1807, a period of thirty-one years, when it was taken away by statute, by reason of unsatisfactory conditions and results.* After the close of the Civil War, the southern states which had gone into rebellion were admitted back into the Union under constitutions limiting suffrage to men. These precedents in our governmental history were never departed from until in recent years.

The greatest danger to the Republic of the United States today, as it always has been in governments where the people rule, is in an excitable and emotional suffrage. If the women of this country would always think coolly and deliberate calmly, if they could always be controlled and act by judgement and not under passion, they might help us to keep our institutions 'eternal as the foundations of the continent itself', but the philosophers of history and the experience of the ages past and present tell us in unanswerable arguments and teach us by illustrations drawn from actual experience that governments have been overturned or endangered in periods of great excitement by emotional suffrage and the speech and writings of intolerant people.

Open that terrible page of the French Revolution and the days of terror, when the click of the guillotine and the rush of blood through the streets of Paris demonstrated to what extremities the ferocity of human nature can be driven by political passion. Who led those bloodthirsty mobs? Who shrieked loudest in that hurricane of passion? Woman. Her picture upon the page of history is indelible. In the city of Paris, in those ferocious mobs, the controlling agency – nay, not agency but the controlling and principal power – came from those whom God had intended to be the soft and gentle angels of mercy throughout the world.

It has been said that if woman suffrage should become universal in the United States, in times of great excitement arising out of sectional questions or local conditions, this country would be in danger of state insurrections and seditions, and that in less than a hundred years revolutions would occur and our republican form of government would come to an end. The United States should guard against emotional suffrage. What we need is to put more logic and less feeling into public affairs. This country has already extended suffrage beyond reasonable bounds. Instead of enlarging it there are strong reasons why it should be curtailed. It would have been better for wise and safe government and the welfare of all the people if there had been some reasonable standard of fitness for the ballot.

During the intense feeling and turbulent conditions growing out of the Civil War, suffrage was so extended that many of the southern states were turned over to the political control of those not sufficiently informed to conduct good government. It has taken half a century of strenuous effort to correct that mistake. The granting of universal woman suffrage would greatly increase the existing evil and put it beyond the possibility of correction except by an ultimate revolution.

We hear it frequently stated that there is no argument against woman suffrage except sentiment. We can reply with equal force that there is no argument for woman suffrage except sentiment, and that often misguided and uninformed. Some suffragists insist that if woman suffrage became universal 'it would set in motion the machinery of an earthly paradise'. It was a woman of high standing in the literary and journalistic field who answered, 'It is my opinion it would let loose the wheels of purgatory.' Suffragists frequently ask the question, 'If we want to vote, why should other people object?' If it is wrong they should not ask it any more than they should ask the privilege of committing a crime. If it is a wrong against the state every other man and woman has a right to object, and it is their duty to object.

There are spheres in which feeling should be paramount. There are kingdoms in which the heart should reign supreme. That kingdom belongs to woman – the realm of sentiment, the realm of love, the realm of gentler and holier and kindlier attributes that make the name of wife, mother and sister next to the name of God himself, but it is not in harmony with suffrage and has no place in government.

We submit these considerations in all candour to the men of this state. Ultimately the decision of this question at the polls is a man's question. We ask your co-operation.

Omaha, 6th July 1914.

JOSEPH H. MILLARD
Ex-US Senator and President of Omaha National Bank
(largest creditor of Willow Springs Distillery)

JOHN A. MCSHANE
Ex-Congressman and retired capitalist

JOHN LEE WEBSTER
Lawyer, representing Omaha Street Railway

LUTHER DRAKE
President of Merchants' National Bank

JOHN C. COWIN
Prominent lawyer

WILLIAM F. GURLEY
Prominent lawyer

WILLIAM D. MCHUGH
Lawyer representing Standard Oil Company

FRANK T. HAMILTON
President of Omaha Gas Co. and officer of Street Railway Co.

WILLIAM WALLACE
Former cashier at Omaha National Bank

JOHN A. MUNROE
Vice-President of Union Pacific Railway Company

FRANK BOYD
Employee of Omaha National Bank

GERRIT FORT
Union Pacific Railway official

JOSEPH BARKER
Insurance official

EDWARD A. PECK
General Manager of Omaha Grain Elevator Company

HENRY W. YATES
President of Nebraska National Bank

MILTON C. PETERS
President of Alfalfa Milling Co.

WILLIAM H. KOENIG
Of firm of Kilpatrick & Co., dry goods merchants

W.H. BOCHOLZ
Vice-President of Omaha National Bank

FRED H. DAVIS
President of First National Bank

BENJAMIN S. BAKER
Lawyer

L.F. CROFOOT
Lawyer for Omaha Smelting Co. and Chicago & Milwaukee RR*

E.E. BRUCE
Wholesale druggist

GEORGE W. HOLDREGE
Manager of Burlington & Missouri River RR Co.

FRED A. NASH
President of Omaha Electric Light Co.

NELSON H. LOOMIS
General Attorney for Union Pacific RR

EDSON RICH
Assistant Attorney for Union Pacific RR

FRANK B. JOHNSON
President of Omaha Printing Co.

THOMAS C. BYRNE
President of Wholesale Dry Goods Co.

REVD THOMAS J. MACKAY
Minister at All Saints' Church (Episcopal)

REVD JOHN W. WILLIAMS
Minister at St Barnabas' Church (Episcopal)

This manifesto, with the signatures, is given almost in full because in language and in the business interests of the signers it is thoroughly typical of the open opposition to woman suffrage. The other classes who were opposed – the 'machine' politicians, the liquor interests and those directly or indirectly connected with them – for the most part worked more secretly.

NOTE ON THE TEXT

The text of this edition is taken from the 'Preface', 'Introduction', 'Chapter 1: Preceding Causes' and 'Appendix' from *The History of Woman Suffrage*, Volume I (1881) and 'Chapter 51: Progress of the Women's Movement in the United Kingdom' and 'Appendix: Nebraska Men's Association Opposed to Woman Suffrage' from *The History of Woman Suffrage*, Volume VI (1922). In some instances, spelling, punctuation and grammar have been silently corrected to make the text more appealing to the modern reader, and names incorrectly spelt have been corrected.

NOTES

11 *Governments… consent of the governed*: A quote from the Declaration of Independence: 'Governments are instituted among Men, deriving their just powers from the consent of the governed'.

11 *Mary Wollstonecraft… Paulina Wright Davis*: For those mentioned in the text, more information is given where they occur: for Mary Wollstonecraft see first

note to p. 52; for Frances Wright see second note to p. 54; for Lucretia Mott see first note to p. 63; for Harriet Martineau see fourth note to p. 52; for Lydia Maria Child see ninth note to p. 58; for Margaret Fuller see third note to p. 52; for Sarah and Angelina Grimké see first note to p. 60; for Harriot K. Hunt see second note to p. 58; for Mariana W. Johnson see sixth note to p. 58; for Ann Preston see second note to p. 58; for Eliza Farnham see third note to p. 62; for Paulina Wright Davis see fourth note to p. 58. Josephine Sophia White Griffing (1814–72) and Martha Coffin Wright (1806–75) were American abolitionists and women's rights activists; the American sisters Alice Cary (1820–71) and Phoebe Cary (1824–71) were poets who worked both together and separately (the spelling 'Phebe' here is presumably taken from a biography of the sisters written by Horace Greeley – see first note to p. 68); Abigail Lydia Mott Moore (1795–1846) was an American abolitionist and women's rights activist; and Lydia Folger Fowler (1823–79) was an American physician and activist, and was the second American woman to earn a medical degree (after Elizabeth Blackwell – see second note to p. 58).

13 this work: i.e. *The History of Woman Suffrage*, Volume I.

13 *Woman Suffrage Movement*: The NAWSA (National American Woman Suffrage Movement).

15 *the most momentous... human race*: In a call for a meeting of the NAWSA, thought to be written by Elizabeth

Cady Stanton, this quote is attributed to the American abolitionist, attorney and activist Wendell Phillips (1811–84).

20 *the State of New York… rights of property*: A reference to the Married Women's Property Act of 1848.

20 *husband and wife… the husband*: A reference to the *Commentaries on the Laws of England* by William Blackstone (1723–80), which states that 'by marriage, the husband and wife are one person in law: that is, the very being or legal existence of the woman is suspended during the marriage.'

21 *the party in power since 1865*: Andrew Johnson (1808–75) was elected President of the United States in 1865, and from then on the United States had a Republican president until 1885. (In fact, Johnson switched to the Democratic party in 1868, in his final year of presidency, but this doesn't seem to be counted here. Also, Johnson was preceded by Abraham Lincoln (President 1861–65), who was also technically a Republican, although this was while the party was known as the National Union Party.)

21 *the thirteenth, fourteenth… Constitution*: The amendments to the US Constitution added extra protections and laws; the first ten were enacted en bloc, and are referred to the Bill of Rights. The thirteenth amendment abolished slavery, the fourteenth defined the rights of citizenship and added 'due process' and 'equal protection' and the fifteenth enfranchised African Americans by prohibiting officials from denying

anyone the right to vote 'on account of race, colour or previous condition of servitude'. The nineteenth amendment, enfranchising women, was not proposed until 1919, and not ratified until 1920.

23 *the majority... an equal*: A quote from the essay *The Subjection of Women* (1869) by the philosopher and politician John Stuart Mill (1806–73).

25 *That little band of heroes... in 1776*: The American Revolution (also known the War of American Independence), stretched from 1775 until 1783. It soon became clear that those heralding American independence from the British as a step forward for humanity didn't intend to grant any protections for slaves; as a result, in November 1775, John Murray, Royal Governor of the British Colony of Virginia, signed Dunmore's Proclamation, which promised freedom to slaves that escaped their masters and went to fight for the British, leading to 1000–2000 slaves taking up arms for the British.

25 *ranked... criminals and minors*: That is, those who were not allowed to vote.

25 *she is made responsible... criminal goes free*: Possibly a reference to rape; abortions were made illegal in many states from 1820.

26 *colleges... their advantages*: The first degree-granting institution in the US, Georgia Female College, opened in 1836, and Catherine Elizabeth Benson (1822–1908) became the first woman to be awarded a bachelor's degree. More and more universities for women opened

in the latter half of the nineteenth century, but there still wasn't widespread enrolment until the early twentieth century. Meanwhile, women still were not allowed to enrol at many of the famous universities – while the first female students arrived at Brown in 1891, Columbia didn't lift the ban for women until 1983.

28 *The elements of sovereignty... power*: A further reference to Blackstone's *Commentaries* (see second note to p. 20).

29 *our late war*: The American Civil War (1861–65).

30 *When England... Geneva Arbitration*: A reference to the *Alabama* Claims of 1869, a series of demands for damages sought by the US from the British for attacks against its ships by Confederate Navy ships that had been built by the British. The claims were settled with a treaty and arbitration in Geneva.

33 *George Eliot... Maria Mitchell*: References to the English writer George Eliot (Mary Ann Evans, 1819–80), the French artist Rosa Bonheur (1822–99), the English poet Elizabeth Barrett Browning (1806–61) and the American astronomer, librarian and educator Maria Mitchell (1818–89).

34 *Order reigns in Warsaw*: A reference to the Battle of Warsaw, fought in September 1831 between Imperial Russia and Poland, in which an attempted liberal revolution was quashed. This quote accompanied myriad caricatures in the international press, depicting the death of liberal values.

35 *The success of a movement... to receive it*: A quote from the introduction to *History of the Rise and Influence of*

the Spirit of Rationalism in Europe, Volume I (1865) by William Edward Hartpole Lecky (1838–1903).

39 *the time of Bunyan*: The main literary output of John Bunyan (1628–88), author of the *Pilgrim's Progress*, was from 1656 onwards.

39 *Lecky... Rationalism in Europe*: See note to p. 35.

39 *Guizot, in his History of Civilisation*: A reference to *Histoire de la civilisation en Europe* (published in French in 1828, translated into English by William Hazlitt in 1846) by François Pierre Guillaume Guizot (1787–1874).

39 *Brahmans... Pariahs*: Brahmans are the highest Hindu caste, traditionally serving as scholars and priests; Pariahs were a low-caste people of southern India, who traditionally functioned as ceremonial drummers.

39 *Herbert Spencer's Descriptive Sociology of England*: A reference to *Descriptive Sociology; or Groups of Sociological Facts* (1873–81) by Herbert Spencer (1820–1903).

41 *A recent writer... ordained of Heaven*: This is now obscure – it is perhaps paraphrased or written from memory.

41 *Gladstone... to woman*: The writer and former Prime Minister (1868–74, 1880–85, 1886–86, 1892–94) William Ewart Gladstone (1809–98) was famously anti-Catholic, and did indeed write such pamphlets, most notably *The Vatican Decrees in Their Bearing on Civil Allegiance* (1874). This is a reference to his comment about the spread of Catholicism in England: 'It is chiefly among women.'

43 *Christine of Pisa*: Christine de Pizan (1364–*c*.1430) was an Italian poet and author at the Court of King Charles VI of France.

43 *Margaret of Angoulême… classic*: Marguerite de Navarre (1492–1549) was a princess of France, Queen of Navarre (a former province, now part of northern Spain) and author. *Heptaméron* is a collection of short stories she wrote, published after her death in 1558 to great acclaim.

43 *Revue des Deux Mondes*: The *Revue* ('Review of Two Worlds') is a French-language magazine, published monthly since 1829.

43 *A paper… Emancipation of Woman*: A reference to the French economist and writer Henri Joseph Léon Baudrillart (1821–92), who wrote, 'Women are given woman to consume, the young are given the young and, in this formal and narcissistic emancipation, their real liberation is successfully averted.'

44 *In 1509… the superiority of woman*: A reference to the German polymath Heinrich Cornelius Agrippa von Nettesheim (1486–1535), who published *Declamatio de nobilitate et praecellentia foeminei sexus* (*Declamation on the Nobility and Preeminence of the Female Sex*) in 1529.

44 *Ruscelli*: Girolamo Ruscelli (1518–66) was a Venetian writer, mathematician and cartographer.

44 *Anthony Gibson… Quality Soever*: Details about the author are now obscure, but the publication details appear to be correct (although the title in full ends: '*Interlarded with Poetry*').

44 *Lucrezia Morinella... Imperfections of Men*: A reference to the Italian poet and author Lucrezia Marinella (1571–1653) and her *La nobiltà et l'eccellenza delle donne, co' diffetti et mancamenti de gli huomini* (1600).

44 *Daniel Defoe... than ourselves*: A reference to *An Essay Upon Projects* (1697), in which Defoe proposes the institution of an academy for women.

45 *Alexander's History... the new age*: A reference to the 1779 work by William Alexander (bap. *c.*1742–*c.*88); the works by Ribera and De Costa are now obscure; a reference to *Women: Their Condition and Influence in Society* (1803) by Alexandre-Joseph-Pierre de Ségur (1756–1805).

45 *Mary Astell and Elizabeth Elstob*: The English philosopher Mary Astell (1666–1731) and the scholar Elizabeth Elstob ('the Saxon Nymph', 1683–1756).

45 *Bishop Burnett*: The Scottish philosopher and Bishop of Salisbury, Gilbert Burnet (1643–1715).

46 *the Conquest*: That is, the Norman Conquest of England in 1066.

46 *The synod of Whitby... Abbess Hilda*: In fact, Hilda of Whitby (*c.*AD 614–80) was the founding abbess of the monastery at Whitby.

46 *famous prophetess... Pope himself*: Sister Elizabeth Barton (1506–34) was executed for her prophecies against the marriage of King Henry VIII and Anne Boleyn.

46 *Ladies of birth... England*: The Witenagemot ('meeting of wise men') was a political apparatus that operated in Anglo Saxon England: a panel of noblemen who advised the king.

46 *In the seventh century... code of laws*: Whightred, King of Kent, assembled the legislature at Baghamstead to put down a new set of laws.

47 *Aula Regia*: 'Royal Hall' (Latin).

47 *Martia*: A reference to Queen Marcia (d. 358 BC), who was, according to Geoffrey of Monmouth, 'one of the most illustrious and praiseworthy of women in early British history', and the third ruler of Britain.

47 *Mrs Ellet... Women of the Revolution*: A reference to *The Women of the American Revolution* (1845) by the American historian Elizabeth Fries Lummis Ellet (1818–77).

47 *Mercy Otis Warren... Corbin*: The references are to the writer Mercy Otis Warren (1728–1814), Abigail Smith Adams (1744–1818), advisor to her husband, John Adams, Jr., and the women's rights advocate Hannah Lee Corbin (1728–*c*.82).

48 *Samuel and John... and Knox*: The Founding Fathers Thomas Jefferson (1743–1826), John Adams (1735–1826), his cousin Samuel (1722–1803), John Dickinson (1732–1808) and Elbridge Gerry (1744–1814). Henry Knox (1750–1806) was a General, a notable figure.

48 *separation*: That is, the 'separation of powers' between the executive, judicial and legislative branches of the government.

49 *Catharine Sawbridge Macaulay*: An English historian, Catharine Macaulay (1731–91), who General Lee met; he recommended her to George Washington, who later said her 'principles are so much and so justly admired by the friends of liberty and mankind'.

49 *Edmund Burke*: A reference to the Anglo-Irish statesman and philosopher Edmund Burke (1729–97), who was an outspoken supporter of American independence.

50 *Bridget Grafford*: The niece of the first President of the Province of New Hampshire, Bridget Grafford (1651–1701) left much land to the town of Portsmouth, including her 'Great Field', for the erection of a school.

51 *Tarleton's*: Sir Banastre Tarleton (1754–1833) was a Lieutenant Colonel in the American War of Independence.

51 *Mrs Brevard's mansion... adopted*: Dr Ephraim Brevard (1744–81) is the reputed author of the Mecklenburg Declaration of Independence (1775); 'Mrs Brevard' is perhaps his wife, Margaret (1744–80).

52 *In 1790... Rights of Women*: Wollstonecraft (1759–97) published *A Vindication of the Rights of Men* in 1790 in response to *Reflections on the Revolution in France* by Edmund Burke (see second note to p. 49); *A Vindication of the Rights of Woman* was published in 1792.

52 *her husband appealed... mankind*: After her death, Wollstonecraft's husband, William Godwin (1756–1836), published a biography of her, *Memoirs of the Author of A Vindication of the Rights of Woman*, in an attempt to clear her name. Unfortunately, in trying to present a rounded view of his wife, he only inflamed the debate, and she became a reviled figure.

52 *Margaret Fuller*: A reference to the American writer and activist Sarah Margaret Fuller Ossoli (1810–50). See also 'Appendix: On Margaret Fuller' on pp. 67–71.

52 *Jane Marcet, Eliza Lynn and Harriet Martineau*: The writers Jane Marcet (1769–1858), Eliza Lynn Linton (1822–98) and Harriet Martineau (1802–76).

52 *Conversations on Chemistry*: Marcet's most famous work, *Conversations on Chemistry, Intended More Especially for the Female Sex*, was published anonymously in 1805.

53 *Mrs Marcet also wrote upon political economy*: A reference to *Conversations on Political Economy*, published in 1816.

53 *Besides her numerous... Westminster Review*: Amongst Martineau's most notable works is *Illustrations of Political Economy* (1834); between 1852 and 1866 she contributed some 1600 articles to the *Daily News*; not only did she contribute articles to the *Westminster Review*, but she was also one of the financial backers that prevented its collapse in 1854.

53 *National Anti-Slavery Standard*: Established in 1840, the *National Anti-Slavery Standard* was a weekly newspaper put out by the American Anti-Slavery Society, which ran until 1870, when the fifteenth amendment to the US Constitution was ratified (see second note to p. 21).

53 *Catharine II*: Catharine the Great (1729–96) was the last reigning Empress of Russia (r. 1762–96).

53 *La Harpe*: Probably Frédéric-César de La Harpe (1754–1838), Swiss political leader, ardent republican and tutor to Alexander I (1777–1825, Emperor 1801–25), grandson of Catharine II, who set in motion policies that eventually led to the abolition of serfdom.

54 *Madame Roland... woman's political rights*: Marie-Jeanne Roland de la Platière (1754–93) was a revolutionary

131

and leading figure in the political group the Girondins; Marie-Anne Charlotte de Corday d'Armont (1768–93) was a political activist who assassinated Jean-Paul Marat (1743–93), who she held responsible for the September Massacres, saying at her trial, 'I have killed one man to save a hundred thousand'; Sophie Lapierre (dates unknown) was an activist, seamstress and teacher who was famed for singing revolutionary anthems at her trial for insurrection; Emmanuel-Joseph Sieyès (1748–1836) and Marie Jean Antoine Nicolas de Caritat, Marquis of Condorcet (1743–1794) were political theorists and philosophers, and at least de Caritat was known for his call for equal rights for men and women of all races.

54 *Frances Wright*: Frances ('Fanny') Wright (1795–1852) was a Scottish-born writer and philosopher.

54 *In 1820 she came… twenty-two years of age*: In fact, Frances made the thirty-day voyage to the US in the summer of 1818, not 1820, so although her given date of birth is incorrect, she was indeed twenty-two at the time.

54 *LaFayette*: In full, Marie-Joseph Paul Yves Roch Gilbert du Motier, Marquis de La Fayette (1757–1834), a French aristocrat who fought in the American Revolution and was a key figure in the French Revolution; he was a friend of Wright's father (a wealthy textile manufacturer and political activist).

55 *The Christian Party in Politics*: Presumably a reference to the Democratic Party, which was founded in 1828. Wright was an outspoken supporter of women's rights,

saying that political progress required the progress of women; she was ostracised for this view, and for her denunciation of slavery, which jarred with the views of many Democrats at the time, particularly in the South.

55 *Mrs Emma Willard*: Emma Hart Willard (1787–1870) was an American women's rights activist and educationalist.

56 *Governor Clinton of New York*: DeWitt Clinton (1769–1828) was a US Senator, Governor of New York (1817–22 and 1825–28) and Mayor of New York City (1803–07, 1808–10, 1811–15).

57 *Motive Power… Harvey's theory*: A reference to her 1846 pamphlet *A Treatise on the Motive Powers which Produce the Circulation of the Blood*. Harvey refers to William Harvey (1578–1657), who was the first to describe the circulation system, in his 1628 pamphlet *Exercitatio anatomica de motu cordis et sanguinis in animalibus* ('*Anatomical Account of the Motion of the Heart and Blood*', Latin).

57 *In 1736… Elizabeth Blackwell*: A reference to the Scottish botanical illustrator and writer Elizabeth Blackwell (*c.*1707–58), whose *A Curious Herbal* (published between 1737 and 1739), which she both wrote and provided the illustrative engravings for, was a groundbreaking reference work on plants from the New World. She married her cousin, Alexander Blackwell (1700–47), a doctor and unsuccessful businessman; although there is no evidence that Elizabeth was put in debtor's prison, her husband certainly was, in no small part due to his business decisions and lavish spending,

leaving her to fend for herself, and, eventually, forcing her to sell some of the rights to her work.

58 *Bunyan prepared... Progress*: See first note to p. 39.

58 *Lady Montague's... Mary Putnam Jacobi*: The references are to: the English aristocrat and writer Lady Mary Wortley Montagu (1689–1762), who was instrumental in introducing a smallpox inoculation to Britain; Marie-Anne Victoire Gillain Boivin (1773–1841), a French midwife and obstetrics writer, whose 1818 work *Nouveau traité des hémorragies de l'utérus* (*'New Treatment for Haemorrhages of the Uterus'*) is probably what is being referred to here; Angélique Marguerite Le Boursier du Coudray (*c.*1712–94), a French midwife who invented the first life-sized obstetrical model ('the machine') for practising mock births; Elizabeth Blackwell, the British physician (1821–1910), who was the first woman to receive a medical degree in the US (not Elizabeth Blackwell the botanical illustrator previously mentioned – see second note to p. 57); and to the early female physicians Harriot Kezia Hunt (1805–75), Clemence Sophia Harned Lozier (1813–88), Ann Preston (1813–72), Hannah E. Longshore (1819–1901), Laura Ross Wolcott (1834–1915), Marie Elisabeth Zakrzewska (1829–1902) and Mary Corinna Putnam Jacobi (1842–1906). Marie Jackson's name appears to have been lost to time, but it is clear from the context that she was a physician whose career flourished in the mid-nineteenth century.

58 *Mary Gove Nichols*: A reference to Mary Sargeant Gove Nichols, known as Mary Orme (1810–84), a women's rights and health reform activist and writer.

58 *Paulina Wright (Davis)*: A reference to Paulina Kellogg Wright Davis (1813–76), an American suffragist later involved in the National Woman Suffrage Association with Susan B. Anthony.

58 *Paulina Wright... in her illustrations*: As showing woman's ignorance and prejudice, Mrs Davis used to relate that when she uncovered her manikin some ladies would drop their veils because of its indelicacy, and others would run from the room; sometimes ladies even fainted (AUTHOR'S NOTE).

58 *Mariana Johnson*: Now obscure, but possibly an alternative name for Mariana Wright Chapman (1843–1907), an American social reformer who was present at the convention of the Woman Suffrage Association in 1884.

58 *Elizabeth Blackwell... diploma at Geneva*: The writer's father, a physician, as early as 1843–44, canvassed the subject of giving his daughter (Matilda Joslyn Gage) a medical education, looking to Geneva – then presided over by his old instructor – to open its doors to her. But this bold idea was dropped, and Miss Blackwell was the first and only lady who was graduated from that institution until its incorporation with the Syracuse University and the removal of the college to that city (AUTHOR'S NOTE).

58 *Dr Samuel Gregory... Medical Education Society*: A reference to Samuel Gregory (1813–72), the founder of the New England Female Medical College.

58 *Lydia Maria Child… History of Woman*: A reference to the women's rights activist Lydia Maria Child (1802–80); it is unclear what work is being referred to here, since Child doesn't seem to have published such a book in 1832. Her most famous work, *The Frugal Housewife* (1829), a collection of recipes and advice for American housewives, was republished in 1832 as *The American Frugal Housewife*, so perhaps this is the book in question.

59 *In 1836, Ernestine L. Rose… Francis Joseph*: Ernestine Louise Rose (1810–92) was an American suffragist; she did indeed emigrate from Poland to the US in 1936, but there is no suggestion that it was due to banishment by Franz Joseph I (1830–1916), Emperor of Austria (r. 1848–1916).

59 *Judge Hurlbut… Human Rights*: Judge Hurlbut, with a lawyer's prejudice, first prepared a paper against the rights of woman. Looking it over, he saw himself able to answer every argument, which he proceeded to do – the result being his *Human Rights* (AUTHOR'S NOTE). This is a reference to Judge Elisha P. Hurlbut (1807–89) and his 1845 *Essay on Human Rights*.

59 *In the winter of 1836… rights of property*: It was not until 1848 that the Married Women's Property Act finally came into force.

59 *similar bills*: In the 'New York' chapter a fuller account of the discussion and action upon these bills will be given (AUTHOR'S NOTE). See *History of Woman Suffrage*, Volume I, Chapter 4: 'New York', pp. 63–87.

60 *Sarah and Angelina Grimké*: The abolitionist and suffragist sisters Sarah Moore Grimké (1792–1873) and Angelina Emily Grimké Weld (1805–79).

60 *Sarah published… will of God*: Probably *Letters on the Equality of the Sexes and the Condition of Woman* (1838).

60 *William Lloyd Garrison… Boston mob*: A prominent abolitionist, William Lloyd Garrison (1805–79) came to the attention of proponents of slavery, and an effigy of him was burned and a gallows set up outside his office in Boston.

60 *In May 1837… delegates*: A reference to the first Anti-Slavery Convention of American Women, held in New York City on the 9th–12th of May 1837.

61 *John Quincy Adams… God*: The statesman John Quincy Adams (1767–1848), President of the United States (1825–29) became increasingly critical of those supporting slavery, particularly those in the Democratic party.

61 *Lydia Maria Child… Isaac T. Hopper*: The references are to the American abolitionists and activists Sarah Pugh (1800–84), Abby Kelley Foster (1811–87), Rebecca Buffum Spring (1811–1911), Abigail Hopper Gibbons (1801–93) and Isaac Tatem Hopper (1771–1852). For Lydia Maria Child see ninth note to p. 58. Mary Grove, Henrietta Sargent, Mary S. Parker, Anne Webster, Deborah Shaw, Martha Storrs and A.L. Cox are now obscure, but given the context, they were clearly abolitionists and suffragists of the day.

62 *In 1840… Woman vs. Man*: This was the article's original title as Fuller (see third note to p. 52) conceived it,

but in the end it was simply titled 'The Great Lawsuit'. It was later published (in 1845) in book form as *Woman in the Nineteenth Century*.

62   *This... as a thinker*: See Appendix (AUTHOR'S NOTE).

62   *Woman and her... Eliza Woodson Farnham*: A reference to the 1864 book by Eliza Farnham (1815–64).

62   *Sing Sing (NY) State Prison*: Sing Sing Correctional Facility in Ossining, New York.

62   *Georgiana Bruce Kirby and Mariana Johnson*: A reference to the American schoolteacher (and friend of Margaret Fuller and Eliza Farnham – see third note to p. 52 and third note to p. 62 respectively) Georgiana Bruce Kirby (1818–87). For Mariana Johnson see sixth note to p. 58.

62   *Revd Samuel J. May*: A reference to the American abolitionist and women's rights activist Samuel Joseph May (1797–1871).

62   *Clarina Howard Nichols, in her husband's paper*: A reference to the American abolitionist, journalist and women's rights activist, Clarina Irene Howard Nichols (1810–85), to whom chapter seven of *History of Woman Suffrage*, Volume I was dedicated ('Reminiscences by Clarina I. Howard Nichols'). She wrote for the *Windham County Democrat*, and married the editor, George Nichols.

63   *Lucretia Mott*: Lucretia Mott (1793–1880) was an American abolitionist and women's rights activist.

63   *Richard H. Dana of Boston*: Richard Henry Dana Jr. (1815–82) was an American lawyer and abolitionist.

63 *Elizabeth Wilson… Martha Bradstreet of Utica*: Both Elizabeth Wilson and Martha Bradstreet are now obscure, although as a footnote in history, a Martha Bradstreet petitioned Congress to investigate Alfred Conkling (1789–1874), United States Representative, so, if it is the same Bradstreet, it seems likely she was a fellow activist.

63 *Antoinette L. Brown*: Antoinette Louisa Brown (1825–1921) was the first ordained Protestant minister in the United States.

63 *Oberlin College… co-education*: Founded in 1833, Oberlin College is a private liberal arts college in Oberlin, Ohio. Not only is it the oldest co-educational college in the United States, admitting women since 1837, it was also one of the first to admit African American students (since 1835).

64 *Lucy Stone*: Lucy Stone (1818–93) was a prominent abolitionist and suffragist.

64 *Elizabeth Heyrick*: A reference to Elizabeth Heyrick (1769–1831), an English abolitionist.

64 *Helene Marie Weber*: A reference to the German politician and activist Helene Weber (1881–1962).

64 *Lady Morgan's Woman and Her Master*: A reference to *Woman and Her Master* (1840) by the Irish writer Sydney, Lady Morgan (bap. 1783–1859).

64 *Appeal of Women… William Thompson*: A reference to the 1825 work *Appeal of One Half of the Human Race, Women, Against the Pretensions of the Other Half, Men* by William Thompson (1775–1833), Anna Wheeler (*c.*1780–1848) and John Stuart Mill (see note to p. 23).

65 *Madam Mathilde Anneke... battlefields of Germany*: A reference to the German writer and radical Mathilde Franziska Anneke (1817–84), who joined the armed group of Friedrich 'Fritz' Anneke (1818–72) – her husband – in support of revolutionary forces in Baden, where she carried messages on the battlefield as described.

65 *The works of... in the camp*: The references are to: the writers Fredrika Bremer (1801–65), Charlotte Brontë (1816–55), Catharine Maria Sedgwick (1789–1867), Harriet Beecher Stowe (1811–96), Felicia Dorothea Hemans (1793–1835) and Lydia Huntley Sigourney (1791–1865); the artists Maria Anna Angelika Kauffmann (1741–1807) and Harriet Goodhue Hosmer (1830–1908); the scientists Mary Somerville (1780–1872) and Caroline Lucretia Herschel (1750–1848); the prison reformers Elizabeth Fry (1780–1845), Dorothea Dix (1802–87) and Mary Carpenter (1807–77); and the nurses and social reformers Florence Nightingale (1820–1910) and Clarissa Harlowe Barton (1821–1912). For George Eliot, Elizabeth Barrett Browning, Rosa Bonheur and Maria Mitchell see note to p. 33.

67 *Ralph Waldo Emerson*: The writer, philosopher and abolitionist Ralph Waldo Emerson (1803–82).

67 *William H. Channing, in her memoirs*: A reference to the clergyman, writer and philosopher William Henry Channing (1810–84), who wrote the *Memoir of Margaret Fuller Ossoli* (1852) with Emerson.

67 *Revd James Freeman Clarke*: A reference to the American theologian and writer James Freeman Clarke (1810–88).

68 *Horace Greeley... of a Busy Life*: A reference to the 1868 work by the American publisher Horace Greeley (1811–72), founder and editor of the *New York Tribune*.

68 *George Ripley*: George Ripley (1802–80) was an American social reformer and journalist.

69 *Her work... Woman vs. Man*: See first note to p. 62.

70 *Theodore Parker*: A reference to the social reformer Theodore Parker (1810–60).

73 *1900–20*: The *History* is indebted for this chapter to Mrs Millicent Garrett Fawcett, JP, LLD (1847–1929), who has been prominently connected with the movement for women's suffrage in Great Britain for nearly fifty years and was President of the National Association from 1904, when it was re-organised, until after the victory was won in 1918 (EDITOR'S NOTE). The 'National Association' is the National Union of Women's Suffrage Societies.

73 *Helen Blackburn*: Helen Blackburn (1842–1903) was an Irish women's rights activist.

73 *the year 1918... franchise for women*: The Representation of the People Act 1918 enfranchised women over the age of thirty who met certain property criteria.

73 *the South African war, 1899–1902*: That is, the (Second) Boer War.

74 *Transvaal... President Kruger*: Stephanus Johannes Paulus Kruger (1825–1904) was President of the South African Republic (Transvaal) from 1883 to 1900.

74 *uitlanders*: A name given to settlers ('outlanders', mainly British) by the Boers.

74 *Women's Suffrage… a Great Movement*: An 1899 work by Fawcett.

74 *Mrs Humphry Ward*: Mary Augusta Ward (1851–1920) was a British writer and educationalist, and was also President of the Women's National Anti-Suffrage League.

76 *The Parliament… Bannerman*: The general election of 1906 gave the Liberal party a landslide majority, and the Conservative party (in full, the Conservative and Unionist Party) lost 246 seats, and with their allies, the Liberal Unionists, ended up with only 157. Sir Henry Campbell-Bannerman (1836–1908) was the leader of the Liberal party and Prime Minister of the United Kingdom from 1905 to 1908.

76 *Mr Herbert H. Asquith, Chancellor of the Exchequer*: Herbert Henry Asquith (1852–1928) was a Liberal politician, and was Prime Minister from 1908 until 1916.

76 *Mr James Bryce*: James Bryce (1838–1922) was a Liberal politician who served as Ambassador to the United States (1907–13) and Chief Secretary for Ireland (1905–07).

76 *The Women's Social… led by Mrs Pankhurst*: The Women's Social and Political Union (WSPU), formed in 1903, was largely overseen by Emmeline Pankhurst (1858–1928) and her daughters, Christabel (1880–1958) and Sylvia (1882–1960).

77 *In the previous February… Commons*: The Liberal politician Willoughby Hyett Dickinson (1859–1943) brought

the Women's Enfranchisement Bill (which would have given the vote to some women) to Parliament on the 8th of March 1907 for its second reading. However, the bill was 'talked out' – opponents of the bill continued the debate beyond the time allowed for voting, so no vote could be undertaken, and the bill therefore failed.

77 *Gladstone... defeated*: A reference to William Ewart Gladstone (1809–98), Liberal politician and Prime Minister (1868–74, 1880–85, 1886–86, 1892–94), and to the Representation of the People Act 1884, which gave the vote to all men paying an annual rental of £10 or holding land valued at £10 or more – but not to women.

77 *The emergence... to the suffrage cause*: Various degrees of 'militancy' was reported on from those linked to the WSPU and suffragette movement, from cutting telephone lines and chaining themselves to railings to sending letter bombs, burning (unoccupied) houses at night (including that of David Lloyd George (1863–1945), Chancellor of the Exchequer), rushing the House of Commons and throwing a hatchet at Prime Minister Asquith in 1912.

78 *constitutional suffragists*: A term frequently used in comparisons with 'militant suffragists'.

80 *the emergence... Snowden*: Although founded in the nineteenth century, the Labour party only took root in the general election of 1906 (see first note to p. 76), when the Labour Representation Committee won 29

seats (in part thought to be due to a secret pact with the Liberals, aimed at losing the Conservatives some of their seats). James Keir Hardie (1856–1915) was one of the founders of the party, and was its leader from 1906 to 1908. Philip Snowden (1864–1937) was a prominent Labour member, and was eventually the party's first Chancellor of the Exchequer, from 1929 to 1931. The party as a whole was in favour of extending the vote, and supported women's right to vote (in fact, Snowden was married to Ethel née Annakin (1881–1951), a campaigner for women's suffrage).

81 *Mr Balfour*: Arthur James Balfour (1848–1930) was a Conservative politician who served as Prime Minister from 1902 to 1905, and went on to be Leader of the Opposition until 1911.

81 *Mr Arthur Henderson*: Arthur Henderson (1863–1935) was a Labour politician, eventually Leader of the Opposition (1931–32).

82 *going into the lobby*: i.e. voted (lobbies, or corridors, run down the sides of the chambers in the House of Parliament, and are used for recording votes).

82 *Earl of Lytton... Hon. Sec*: A reference to the Conservative politician Victor Alexander George Robert Bulwer-Lytton (1876–1947), an advocate for women's suffrage, and Henry Noel Brailsford (1873–1958), a left-wing journalist and founding member of the Men's League for Women's Suffrage.

87 *a book by myself called... and After*: In full: *The Women's Victory – and After: Personal Reminiscences, 1911–18.*

88 *Sir Edward Grey*: Edward Grey (1862–1933) was a Liberal politician.

89 *On the 23rd of January... re-introduced*: In around 1912, Asquith reluctantly agreed to allow MPs to vote freely on an amendment to a pending reform bill, which would allow women the vote on the same terms as men. The Speaker of the House, James William Lowther (1855–1949), a Conservative politician, ruled that the amendment changed the nature of the bill, and it would therefore have to be withdrawn.

89 *He was manifestly confounded... Speaker's ruling*: Asquith reportedly had strong words at the time for the Speaker, but is thought not to have been disappointed by the ruling.

91 *Mr John Redmond*: John Edward Redmond (1856–1918) was an Irish nationalist politician, and leader of the Irish Parliamentary Party.

92 *Lord Selborne*: A reference to the Liberal politician William Waldegrave Palmer, 2nd Earl of Selborne (1859–1942).

95 *Dr Elsie Inglis*: Elsie Maud Inglis (1864–1917) was a Scottish doctor and suffragist.

95 *Life of Dr E. Inglis by Lady Frances Balfour*: Lady Frances Balfour (1858–1931), an aristocrat and suffragist (married to Eustace James Anthony Balfour (1854–1911), the younger brother of Arthur Balfour – see first note to p. 81), wrote several biographies, including that of Dr Elsie Inglis, published in 1920.

95 *Royaumont Abbey*: A former Cistercian abbey near Asnières-sur-Oise in Val-d'Oise, about twenty miles north of Paris.

96 *the heroic death of Edith Cavell... October 1915*: Edith Louisa Cavell (1865–1915) was a British nurse who is credited with saving the lives of soldiers from both sides during the war, and for helping around two hundred Allied soldiers escape from German-occupied Belgium. She was arrested for treason and sentenced to death by a German firing squad.

98 *Lord Robert Cecil*: Edgar Algernon Robert Gascoyne-Cecil (1864–1958) was Parliamentary Under-Secretary of State for Foreign Affairs from 1915 to 1919.

98 *Sir Charles Hobhouse, Mr J.A. Pease*: Two Liberal politicians in Asquith's cabinet, Sir Charles Edward Henry Hobhouse (1862–1941) and Joseph Albert Pease (1860–1943).

100 *Mr Walter Long*: Walter Hume Long (1854–1924) was a British Unionist politician.

101 *Sir John Simon... Willoughby Dickinson*: John Allsebrook Simon (1873–1954) was a British politician, initially a Liberal. At this time he was Home Secretary. Willoughby Hyett Dickinson (1859–1943) was a Liberal politician, Member of Parliament for St Pancras North (1906–18).

102 *The Common Cause, the official organ of the NUWSS*: A weekly publication supporting the National Union of Women's Suffrage Societies, published 1909–20.

103 *The Government whips had not been put on*: i.e. MPs were free to vote as they chose, rather than as dictated by their party.

105 *Lord Curzon*: George Nathaniel Curzon (1859–1925) was a Conservative politician and former Viceroy of India (1899–1905).

105 *The Lord Chancellor (Lord Finlay)*: Robert Bannatyne Finlay (1842–1929) was a British doctor and politician, and was Lord High Chancellor of Great Britain from 1916 to 1919.

105 *Lord Lansdowne… Lord Milner*: The references are to: Henry Charles Keith Petty-Fitzmaurice, 5th Marquess of Lansdowne (1845–1927), who held senior positions in both the Liberal and Conservative Party governments; Hardinge Stanley Giffard, 1st Earl of Halsbury (1823–1921), a Conservative and former Lord High Chancellor (1885–86, 1886–92, 1895–1905); Alexander Hugh Bruce, 6th Lord Balfour of Burleigh (1849–1921), a Scottish Unionist; Randall Thomas Davidson (1848–1930), Archbishop of Canterbury from 1903 to 1928; Arthur Foley Winnington-Ingram (1858–1946), Bishop of London from 1901 to 1939; Leonard Henry Courtney (1832–1918), a Liberal politician; and Alfred Milner (1854–1925), a Liberal politician. For Lord Bryce see third note to p. 76; for Lord Selborne see note to p. 92; for Lord Lytton see second note to p. 82.

106 *Lord Sydenham*: George Sydenham Clarke (1848–1933) was a British army officer whose name was tarred with the anti-Semitic and racist pamphlets he wrote, such as *The World Jewish Problem*, published by the pro-Fascist group the Britons.

109 *Miss Eleanor Rathbone*: Eleanor Florence Rathbone (1872–1946) was a politician and activist, and was an independent MP for the Combined English Universities from 1929 until her death in 1946.

109 *In 1907*: Accompanying this chapter was a complete list of laws in the interest of women enacted by the Parliament beginning in 1902, prepared by Miss Chrystal Macmillan, MA, BSc. The lack of space which has compelled the omission of similar laws from all of the state chapters makes it necessary in this one. Three of importance politically are given. (EDITOR'S NOTE.) Jessie Chrystal Macmillan (1872–1937) was a barrister, and was one of the founders of the Women's International League for Peace and Freedom. (Her postnominal letters acknowledge that she was the first female science graduate from the University of Edinburgh.)

109 *the Countess Markievicz*: Constance Georgine Markievicz (1868–1927) was an Irish politician and suffragist, and was the first woman elected to the Westminster Parliament.

110 *Viscountess Astor*: Nancy Witcher Langhorne Astor (1879–1964) was a Conservative politician and MP (1919–45).

111 *Miss Penrose of Somerville College, Oxford*: Dame Emily Penrose (1858–1942) was Principal of Somerville College, Oxford University from 1907 until 1926.

111 Miss B.A. Clough of Newnham College, Cambridge: Blanche Athena Clough (1861–1960) was Principal of Newnham College (1920–23), and was the daughter of the first Principal of Newnham, Anne Jemima Clough (1820–92, Principal 1871–92).

111 Cambridge... open its doors: Although women were first admitted to Girton College in 1869, it wasn't until 1948 that the institution awarded degrees to women.

115 True... conditions and results: The Declaration of Independence proclaimed, 'all men are created equal'. In most states this was interpreted as 'all wealthy white men are created equal', but when New Jersey's first constitution was adopted (in July 1776), the right to vote was given to all 'inhabitants' who had property worth a certain amount. However, in 1807, a law was passed limiting the right to vote to white men.

119 RR: Shorthand for 'railroad'.

INDEX

Macaulay, Catharine Sawbridge, 49
Markievicz, Countess, 109
Marcet, Jane, 52–53
Married Women's Property Act, 20, 59
Martia (see 'Queen Marcia')
Martineau, Harriet, 11, 52–53
May, Samuel J., 62
Memoir of Margaret Fuller Ossoli (see also 'Channing'), 67
Militant (see 'Suffragette')
Mill, John Stuart, 23, 64
Milner, Alfred, 105
Mitchell, Maria, 33, 65
Montagu, Lady Mary Wortley, 58
Morgan, Sydney, Lady, 64
Morinella, Lucrezia, 44
Mott, Lucretia, 11, 63
Mott, Lydia, 11

National American Woman Suffrage Movement (NAWSA), 13
National Anti-Slavery Standard, 53
Nationalists, 75, 81, 87, 99
National Trade Union Congress, 92
National Union of Societies for Equal Citizenship (NUSEC), 109
National Union of Women's Suffrage Societies (NUWSS), 80–81, 85–87, 90–91, 93–96, 99, 102, 104, 108–09
National Woman's Anti-Slavery Convention, 60
Nebraska Men's Association, 113–120
New York Tribune, The, 70

Nichols, Clarina Howard, 62
Nightingale, Florence, 65
Nobleness and Excellence of Women, Together with the Faults and Imperfections of Men, The (see 'Morinella')
Nouveau traité des hémorragies de l'utérus (New Treatment for Haemorrhages of the Uterus) (see also 'Boivin'), 58

Otis, James, 47–48

Palmer, William Waldegrave, 92, 98, 105–06
Pankhurst, Emmeline, 76
Pariah (see 'Caste')
Parker, Mary S., 61
Parker, Theodore, 70
Parliament, 45–46, 73, 75–76, 82, 86–87, 92, 97–100, 102, 104, 108–11
Pease, J.A., 98
Petty-Fitzmaurice, Henry, 105
Phillips, Wendell, 15
Pilgrimage, the, 91
Pilgrim's Progress (see also 'Bunyan'), 58
Pisa, Christine of, 43
Polish Revolution, 65
Pope, the, 18, 38, 46
Preston, Ann, 11, 58
Pugh, Sarah, 61
Punch, 90

Qualification of Women Act, 109
Queen Anne, 45
Queen Elinor, 46
Queen Elizabeth I, 45

OTHER CLASSIC NON-FICTION FROM
RENARD PRESS

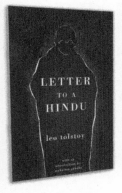

ISBN: 9781913724016
48pp • Pamphlet • £5

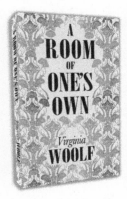

ISBN: 9781913724009
160pp • Paperback • £7.99

ISBN: 9781913724306
60pp • Paperback • £5

ISBN: 9781913724047
64pp • Paperback • £6.99

ISBN: 9781913724733
224pp • Paperback • £7.99

ISBN: 9781913724702
128pp • Paperback • £5.99

DISCOVER THE FULL COLLECTION AT
WWW.RENARDPRESS.COM